PENGUIN BO
HALF A MILLION

David Howe was born in Manchester. After a spell as a school-teacher, he worked first as a child-care officer and then as a social worker. He has studied at the universities of Durham and Nottingham. Since 1976 he has taught at the University of East Anglia in Norwich where he obtained his PhD. and is now a Professor. He is the author of a number of books, including *The Consumers' View of Family Therapy*, published in 1989.

Phillida Sawbridge was born in Bristol. After training and working in child care, she specialised mainly in homefinding for children with special needs. She worked in adoption from 1967 to 1994, when she retired from her post as director of the Post-Adoption Centre in London. She has contributed to many journals and books on adoption, and lectured in Australia and the USA as well as all over Great Britain.

Diana Hinings was born in Birmingham. She graduated in sociology from Leeds University and subsequently qualified as a social worker. She has practised in the field of adoption both in England and the USA. She is currently a lecturer at the University of East Anglia.

HALF A MILLION WOMEN

MOTHERS WHO LOSE
THEIR CHILDREN BY ADOPTION

———————

DAVID HOWE, PHILLIDA SAWBRIDGE
and DIANA HININGS

First published by Penguin Books 1992

This edition published by

The Post-Adoption Centre
5 Torriano Mews, Torriano Avenue
London NW5 2RZ

Charity registration No. 294998

CONTENTS

CONTENTS

Acknowledgements

We are extremely grateful to all the mothers who told us their story. They gave generously of their time; they offered us their views; they wished us well. This book would not have been possible without their kind and considerable help.

The work of the Post-Adoption Centre was the seed-bed out of which our thoughts grew. As the Centre's work is wholly a team venture, we are delighted to record our thanks for the helpful comments and constant encouragement of our colleagues.

Few books see the light of day without the patient efforts of a skilled typist. Anne Borrett produced draft and final copies of the manuscript with her usual speed and accuracy and she receives our full gratitude.

Permissions

The authors and publisher would like to thank a number of publishers for their kind permission to reproduce extracts from the following: *Living Mistakes: Mothers Who Consented to Adoption* by Kate Inglis (Allen & Unwin/Harper Collins Publishers, 1984); *Single and Pregnant* by Sally Macintyre (Croom Helm/Routledge, 1977); *Adoption Today: Change and Choice in New Zealand* by Jenny Rockel and Murray Ryburn (Heinemann Reed, 1988); *The Adoption Triangle* by Arthur D. Sorosky, Annette Baran and Reuben Pannor (Anchor/Doubleday Press, 1978).

Every effort has been made to trace all the copyright-holders, but if any have been overlooked, the publishers will be pleased to make an acknowledgement at the first opportunity.

I
Explaining the Unmarried Mother

Most women who have given up a child for adoption say that it was the most difficult decision they had ever had to make in their lives.

If you are young, unmarried and accidentally pregnant, you are likely to be in a dilemma. Whichever way you turn you will fall foul of some moral standard, you will upset someone close to you. To be pregnant you must have had sexual intercourse outside the sanctity of marriage. Keep the baby and you may be accused of failing to give your child a proper start in life, never mind ruin your education, career, marriage prospects and the best years of your life. Place the baby for adoption and you may feel that you have failed as a mother, indeed failed as a woman. People may eye you critically, rebuking the selfishness of your decision as you give up your baby and struggle to piece together your shattered emotions and the fragments of your old life. You can't win. It is hardly surprising, therefore, that most women who have given up a child for adoption found the decision extremely hard and painful to make.

This much we know. But what happens to women who relinquish a child for adoption? Until recently, remarkably little was known about their fate once they had lost the child. Thinking on modern adoption has gone through two stages. In the first, adoption was to satisfy the needs of the childless married woman. In the second, the philosophy was reversed and it was the needs of the child that were given prime consideration. Couples were chosen for what they could offer the child and not for what the child would give them. But the needs of the mother who gave birth to the child were rarely considered, or, if they were, it was often assumed that her interests were served by relieving her of the infant and providing him or her with a good home and loving parents. Once the child had been placed with adopters, it was the story of the new family that was followed. The focus of interest became the adopted child and how he or she fared in life. The biological mother faded from view. She was forgotten, even denied. She was the neglected corner of the adoption triangle. Not until the child started to ask about his or her origins did the mother reappear, but her image was frozen in time. The last occasion she was seen by either the adopters or their social worker was at the moment of placement.

We have no word for the woman who surrenders her child for adoption. This is unusual in the world of human relationships which has a rich and evocative vocabulary. We speak of lovers and mistresses, Lotharios and strumpets, putative fathers and stepmothers, single parents and orphans, but there is no simple word for the woman who gives up her baby to be reared by another. The absence of a name is further evidence that once the child is adopted, the mother is expected to do the decent thing and disappear from the picture. Her silence is required. The most selfless act she can perform on behalf of her child is to let go and forget all about him or her. And once the child has been surrendered, she has no further role, and she is therefore left without a name. She is a mother who has no baby, and that is no mother at all. 'Natural mother' was used for a while but adopters objected, arguing, with some good cause, that once the child was with the new family, the adoptive mother became that child's natural mother, with the added suspicion that a woman who did not look after her own child had no right to call herself a 'natural' mother, the act of surrendering an infant being a wholly 'unnatural' thing for a mother to do. The current fashion is to call the relinquishing parent the child's 'birth mother'. This does not have a particularly distinctive ring, for all women who have had a child are birth mothers. Nevertheless, in spite of the tautology it commits, we shall use the title as it has the advantage of being relatively short and it is used in professional circles.

But giving women who lose a child by adoption a name is only the first step in our journey to recover their story and bring their experiences into focus. The life of the birth mother all too often remains anonymous and obscure. The rest of this book aims to give the birth mother a voice, to acknowledge her experience, to explain her circumstances and, perhaps most important, to understand her and what she has to say.

HALF A MILLION WOMEN

In the United Kingdom there are at least half a million women who have given up a child for adoption. It is generally agreed that there are around 750,000 adopted people in the country, ranging from the very young to the very old. Half a million birth mothers is therefore a conservative estimate, and many people quote higher figures of 600,000 and more. On these estimates, we calculate that roughly *one woman in twenty-five* in the population has had a child adopted. The proportion will be even higher for older women, for the number of children adopted was greater when they were young and of childbearing age.

The numbers, however, continue to change, reflecting major shifts in the way we view the family and illegitimacy, and rear our children. Adoptions by 'strangers' – people not biologically related to the child – reached an all-time peak in 1968 with 16,164 adoption orders granted in England and Wales. Seventy-six per cent of these were for babies aged under one year. Or put another way, for every thousand babies born live in 1968, fifteen had been adopted by the time they had reached their first birthday. But since that year, the number of children placed for adoption has fallen steadily. In 1984 (the last year in which government departments produced adoption statistics in any useful detail), 4,189 adoption orders were granted, though only 43 per cent were for babies. For every thousand babies born live in that year, only three were adopted before they were one year old.

At first sight, this trend is puzzling. The number and proportion of babies born 'outside marriage' has increased over recent years. For example, in 1970, there were 64,744 (8 per cent) illegitimate births. Thirteen per cent of these children were adopted before they were one year old. But by 1984, there were 110,465 (17 per cent) births outside marriage, though only 1½ per cent of these babies were adopted in their first year of life. By 1987 the proportion of babies born to women who were not married had risen to 23 per cent.

Not only do we see an increase in the number of children born to unmarried women, but we hear a change in their name. For centuries they were simply described as 'bastards', before a more genteel and law-minded society began to call them 'illegitimate'.

Only in the last few years have official records used the phrase 'birth outside marriage' to describe children born to single women, a term which echoes the slightly quaint 'born out of wedlock'. Changes in name reflect changes in the practice of family life. Today, the social stigma attached to the unmarried mother and her child is still present, though less severe. So, for example, established couples who remain unmarried but have children find that their child's birth is recorded as 'outside marriage'. Many women now decide, consciously and deliberately, to become single parents, and their children too will be reported as born outside marriage. The social climate surrounding 'children born out of wedlock' is much more tolerant and accepting. This both encourages women to have babies without necessarily feeling the need to marry and to keep them if they are without a steady partner. In such ways has the number of children born outside marriage risen while the number of babies relinquished for adoption has fallen.

However, at the same time that more permissive attitudes are developing towards sexual relationships and forms of family life, disquiet has increased about the possible dangers that some children may suffer at the hands of their parents. More children than ever are being investigated by social workers as fears about physical, sexual and emotional abuse rise in the minds of the public, the speeches of politicians, the pens of the press, the dispositions of magistrates and the diagnoses of doctors. More and more children are removed from the care of parents by local-authority agents as they respond to pressures from the public, and a growing proportion of these forcibly removed children are being placed for adoption against their mothers' wishes. Of those children adopted today, an increasing number are aged four, five and over at the time they are first placed with their new parents. As the number of unwed mothers who choose to place their babies for adoption continues to fall, the number of mothers whose children are compulsorily removed and placed for adoption against their wishes is increasing. The moral climate that deemed the unmarried woman unfit to be a mother has shifted and we now have a new group of 'unfit' mothers. In a variety of ways these mothers fail to convince social workers and courts that they are competent or safe parents. In their attempts to give a child a secure and permanent home, welfare workers may ask the courts to 'free' the child for adoption. Mothers who fight this nightmarish decision and lose, not only experience all the pain felt by mothers who voluntarily relinquish their baby, they suffer the added horror' of having their children forcibly removed and adopted against their wishes.

CULTURAL CONTEXTS

The changing pattern of adoption practices over the last thirty years tells us that there is nothing fixed or absolute about society's attitude to sex, procreation and parenthood. This observation is important because it allows us to recognize two cultural dimensions that define the way a woman experiences having a baby outside marriage and the way she feels about giving up that child for adoption. The first dimension describes how a particular community regards and interprets the unmarried mother and the practice of adoption. Adoption may be common or rare, it may be handled furtively or it may be treated in an open and matter-of-fact fashion. The second dimension arises out of the first. The way the host society views adoption will strongly influence the mother's experience of and feelings about giving up her child to another set of parents. Generally, the more relaxed, open and fluid the practice of adoption, the less upsetting and stressful does the birth mother find the experience. When we add the two dimensions together, we see that the social context affects both the decision to surrender the child and the extent to which the decision is experienced as a painful loss. The birth mother understands what she has to do and what she has done in the language and ideas of her day.

Adoption practices have varied over time and across cultures. Many theories have been developed to explain why some women have children outside marriage and then place them for adoption. Consideration of the cultural context and the ideas that people have about adoption adds a useful perspective which helps us understand the experiences of the contemporary birth mother.

In order to make sense of adoption, it is first necessary to know something of a society's attitude towards women who have a child outside marriage. If a community is fairly relaxed about an unmarried woman having a child and is willing to support the mother, she will most likely decide to look after the baby herself. According to Pinchbeck (1954) people in medieval Britain did not regard illegitimate children as a problem. They were absorbed by the mother's own community. There were few sanctions and little stigma attached to the unmarried woman who bore a child. The one major drawback for the child born out of marriage was that he or she could not inherit, but with the growing practice of primogeniture, in which only the eldest child inherited, this disadvantaged legitimate children, apart from the first, every bit as much as those who were illegitimate.

Punishing the Unmarried Mother and Her 'Child of Sin'

This climate of acceptance did not last and the lot of the unmarried mother and her child slowly began to change. Money and morals became the yardsticks by which illegitimacy began to be measured and it fell short on both counts. As social and economic arrangements changed under the impact of capitalism, family members who once might have been an asset in the domestic economy or useful in working the land became a liability if they could not gain paid employment in the factories. Children, the sick and the old were dependants and therefore a drain on the family's income. Rearing children became a potential burden which fell entirely on the parents. The extended family was no longer a resource or source of support. Parents, therefore, only felt responsible for their own children; the community was beginning to lose the social mechanisms that had previously allowed dependent members to be cared for without feeling stigmatized. 'In such a society,' observes Tizard, 'people give a very different amount of care and affection to their "own" and to other people's children, and a child without his "own" parents is seriously disadvantaged' (1977, p.2). If the unmarried mother could not be helped to look after her child, in effect that child, in the hands of the parish and the Poor Law, was treated as parentless and dependent, and therefore profoundly disadvantaged.

And on the moral front, the ethics of sixteenth-century Puritanism spread their unflinching way into all corners of life. The prevalence of unmarried mothers and illegitimate babies was

6

taken as an index of the moral state of the community. Churches developed a sterner and more restrictive view of relationships between the sexes. Sexual passion was seen as the 'original sin' and the only arrangement in which it was allowed expression was in the state of 'holy matrimony'. Sexual intercourse outside marriage was morally wrong and therefore any child conceived by an unmarried woman was viewed as 'the wages of sin'. Stigma, shame and guilt were now attached to both the unmarried woman and her child. Morally and economically, illegitimacy was defined as a problem and Pinchbeck, quoting from the preamble to the Poor Law Act of 1576, nicely captures the feelings of the time:

> Concerning bastards begotten and born out of lawful matrimony (an offence against God's and Man's laws) the said bastards being now left to be kept at the charge of the parish where they were born, to be the great burden of the same parish and in defrauding of the relief of the impotent and aged true poor of the same Parish, and to the evil example and the encouragement of the lewd life, it is ordered and enacted.
>
> (Pinchbeck, 1954, p.315)

Such legislation viewed most severely any sexual relationship outside marriage and any child of that relationship. It was intent on penalizing and stigmatizing the unmarried mother, bolstering the institution of marriage and reducing the costs of illegitimate children on the parish. Indeed, bearing an illegitimate child became a serious offence against the community, particularly if the cost of caring for that mother and her baby fell on to the parish:

> Every lewd woman which shall have any bastard which may be chargeable to the parish, the justices of the peace shall commit such woman to the house of correction, to be punished and set on work, during the term of one whole year.
>
> (The statute of 7 James, cap.4 [1610], quoted by Macfarlane, 1980, p.73)

The belief was that the Poor Law had to be harsh and humiliating otherwise the poor would abandon their children with even greater readiness than already was the case. Thus, it was in the interests of both Church and state to take a very dim view of illegitimacy.

'Over the next two hundred years,' writes Gill, 'the severity of sanctions against illegitimate reproduction were increased as society came to acknowledge that stable relationships between parents were "a *sine qua non* of a stable society"' (1977, p.210). By the nineteenth century, the plight of the unmarried mother was extreme. She was condemned morally and spiritually, and punished socially and materially. The harshness of the Bastardy Clauses of the 1834 Poor Law Amendment Act were said to be responsible for a great increase in infanticide because of the impossible life that unmarried mothers were forced to lead, in spite of the fact that such a crime was punished by the death penalty:

> That whereas many lewd women, having been delivered of bastard children, to avoid the shame, and to escape punishment, do secretly bury or conceal the death of their children, and allege after the child has been found dead that she said the child was born dead, it is enacted that if any woman privately, either by herself, or others, conceals the death of a bastard child, she, upon conviction, shall suffer death; unless she shall prove by one witness that the child was born dead.
>
> (The Act of 1832, to Prevent the Destroying and Murdering of Bastard Children [Statute 21, James I, Chapter 27], quoted Gill, 1977, p.216)

However, the commissioners continued to defend the Poor Law, arguing that its severity had lessened the number of illegitimate births and in so doing had improved public morals. Adoption was heavily discouraged as it was tantamount to giving poor 'lewd' women a licence to indulge their sexual passions with impunity. The unmarried mother must suffer the full consequences of her actions. At the age of three, the child would be separated from his or her mother. Only one visit a month was allowed. Many children were sent to live with foster parents, often outside their home area. This made any regular contact with either mother or relatives difficult and thereby acted as an emotional incentive for extended families to look after their own illegitimate children lest they never saw them again.

Overcrowding and Temptations of the Flesh

As the nineteenth century advanced, voices were raised, which if not absolving the unmarried mother from all blame, nevertheless began to recognize that circumstances not of her own choosing often put the young woman in the way of severe temptation. The harsh conditions under which many of the poor lived brought the sexes into close proximity. Overcrowding forced men and women to lose all sense of decency and propriety. Gill (1977, pp.226–7) quotes from the draft report of James Charles, written on the subject of illegitimacy and presented to the Presbytery of Wigtown in June 1864. It was agreed that no single cause accounted for 'the evil', but among those enumerated were:

> Defective housing accommodation. Not a few of the poorer or even the labouring classes have only one apartment, in which fathers, mothers and grown-up children live in common. In such circumstances decency cannot possibly be maintained, and the natural feelings of modesty, which are the safeguards of purity, are soon broken down, or rather are crushed and smothered from the first. The evil is seen in yet more aggravated form in some of the smaller farm houses, where, from scantiness of accommodation, the man-servant and the maid-servant are made to sleep in the same room or closet in beds not far apart from each other!

Although it was generally felt that the moral standards of the poor had become blunted and debased, so that 'the evil' was not even recognized or acknowledged as a shameful and degrading thing, one of the methods of reducing the number of illegitimate births was to improve the quality of housing enjoyed by the poor. Factors other than the spiritual condition of the unmarried mother were accepted as possible causes of the problem of illegitimacy. However, Gill reminds us that the Victorian middle classes *presumed* that those who lived and slept cheek by jowl would automatically engage in unrestricted sexual intercourse. Behind their outrage lay an unease, fear, even abhorrence of human

9

sexuality that was probably not true for the labouring classes themselves, who had a much more robust and relaxed attitude to courting and sexual relationships. For the middle classes, sex inside marriage was just thinkable so long as intercourse was not accompanied by enjoyment. Marital sex was a duty, particularly for women, a duty that had to be endured, though the evidence is strong that something of a double standard operated that turned a blind eye to men enjoying sex outside marriage but not women. The middle classes projected their disquiet on to the lives of the poor, who were thought to be more susceptible to the sins of the flesh. The working class's less inhibited attitude to sex was viewed by the middle classes as a dangerous threat to the established order of society (ibid., p.171). Sexual relations outside marriage, never mind becoming an unmarried mother, were defined as a social problem about which something had to be done. The unmarried mother and her bastard child threatened both the idea and the ideal of marriage. Therefore mother and child had to be condemned, legally, materially and morally. The only softening of the moral line was to regard women who became pregnant as mentally dull and unable to protect themselves against persistent, plausible and unprincipled men. Young (1954, p.5) notes that in the late nineteenth century a number of European countries passed local laws providing automatic guardianship for all illegitimate children on the grounds that women who became pregnant outside marriage must be intellectually incapable of planning for them.

In their critical approach to the Victorian middle classes, historians and sociologists began to see the unmarried mother neither as a moral degenerate nor simply a victim of her overcrowded environment, but rather as someone who was part of a community, a culture if you will, in which standards of behaviour differed from those of the middle classes and yet made sense in terms of the economic and social conditions in which the poor had to live. In many countries and different cultures, children born outside marriage were accepted as part of 'the way of life'. The 'problem' of illegitimacy was in the eyes of middle-class beholders, but it was their view that continued to determine the way the unmarried mother was treated.

The Adoption Act of 1926

It has been estimated that in the years prior to the First World War, at any one time around 80,000 children were in residential care under the provisions of the Poor Law. It was also recognized that in the majority of cases, the child produced by these large institutions was a sad figure, described by Benet as 'unlovable, uncooperative, and all but unemployable' (1976, p.73). This argued for legal adoption as a better way of bringing up these children, which, when coupled with the growing demand of the childless middle-class woman to adopt, seemed to produce an unassailable case. Even so, there was a reluctance on the part of politicians to take the issue forward and the old fears that adoption would only encourage some women into a life of sexual promiscuity were still heard. It took the First World War and the need to provide orphaned children with decent homes to tip the balance in favour of legalizing adoption. The Adoption Act of 1926 allowed a woman to have her child brought up by another set of parents as if the child was their own. Many years later, the Houghton Report was to define adoption as 'the complete severance of the legal relationship between parents and child and the establishment of a new one between the child and his adoptive parents' (1972, p.4). It was assumed that the birth mother would not want to have any form of contact with her child or learn of his or her progress and there was certainly no mechanism to facilitate it. The break was meant to be clean and absolute. The child was to be reared as if he or she was the biological child of the adoptive parents. This was felt to be in the best interests of all concerned. It allowed the birth mother to make a fresh start. It was probably thought good that adopted children did not inquire too deeply into their background, as most were the illegitimate offspring of poor working-class women. The origins of many adopted children continued to remain shrouded in secrecy and shame.

From Morals to Mind: Psychological Perspectives
on the Unwed Mother

The twentieth century continued to regard illegitimacy as a social problem. And as the central character in this problem, the unmarried mother continued to need explanation. Why, as a young unmarried woman, did she engage in sexual intercourse and, even more puzzling, why did she allow herself to get pregnant? As the intellectual climate continued to change so did the models of explanation. So long as her behaviour was seen as immoral and a threat to social stability, it was likely that she would be punished for her sins. But there were those who believed that the unmarried mother was as much a product of her poor, mean and overcrowded environment as she was of her wicked ways. So rather than punish her, the problem of illegitimacy might be cured by improving her material circumstances. And if this did not work, then the stage was set for the next explanatory step: her behaviour was the result of a sick psychology, an immature personality, a disturbed mind. The unmarried mother was a psychiatric case who needed treatment. Her behaviour was morally inexcusable, but it was no longer appropriate for her to be punished. Science gradually began to replace ethics as the basis on which to explain and, more importantly, treat the unwed mother. It was no longer her body and what she had done with it that were the object of punishment but rather the quality of mind that needed attention. So, though not guilty of a moral lapse, the unmarried mother was still regarded as a deviant:

> In this phase of social scientific thinking bastardy was taken as a prime example of something which interrupted the proper functioning of social processes and revealed a failure of social control, the control of individual behaviour by family and kin, by political and education authority, by all influences which persuade most people to obey established norms. The conditions which were associated with high illegitimacy levels in any one locality tended to be thought of as pathological, and the individuals who engendered bastards as in some way victimized, disordered, even mentally disordered.

> (Laslett, 1980, pp.1–2)

By the 1940s and 1950s, elaborate psychological models existed which sought to explain why some unmarried women had babies; the daughter was 'acting out' her mother's promiscuous wishes; the adolescent girl was testing her body's sexual potency; a baby could be used as a transitional object to ease the process of separation of daughter from mother; the baby is an object that can be loved by mothers who themselves have felt unloved as children. Most pregnant teenagers were thought to be the product of families undergoing some stress and turbulence: 'when an adolescent girl in our society becomes pregnant outside of wedlock this is indicative that something has gone wrong in the relationship between the girl and her parents' (Rall, 1961, p.3). One way for the adolescent child to resolve such conflicts, particularly with her parents, is to act impulsively. This allows Mary Rall to write, with not a hint of a smile, that 'when a boy or girl yields to the sexual impulse before he or she is ready to assume the responsibilities, and experience the gratifications inherent in a mutually satisfying marital relationship and in parenthood, we need to understand what has gone wrong' (1961, p.3). The young woman hopes to use her pregnancy as a 'solution' to her difficult family situation. Her pregnancy, therefore, is the symptom of emotional disturbance. There is a psychopathological reason, often unconsciously formed, for any young unmarried woman finding herself pregnant. The work of Leontine Young provides the classic illustration of the unwed mother as an emotionally disturbed young woman.

Young believes that there is nothing haphazard or accidental in becoming an unwed mother. The girl's behaviour is purposeful, she is determined, 'however unconscious, to have not just a baby but specifically a baby out of wedlock' (1945, reproduced in Roberts, ed., 1966, p.82). There is a drive for the girl to have a baby without having a man. Her behaviour is compulsive and to say that it 'is the result of immorality or free choice is to ignore all the evidence . . . The logical and seemingly inevitable result of her psychological development is an out-of-wedlock child, and, like a sleepwalker, she acts out what she must do without awareness or understanding of what it means . . .' (Young, 1954, p.36). The 'girls' were nearly all found to come from three general types of family pattern and it was this pattern which determined the girl's personality and therefore the likelihood of her getting pregnant. In particular, it was felt that the girl's relationship with one or both of her parents was the origin of her motivation to become pregnant.

The belief that the unwed mother's pregnancy was rooted in a pathological personality led those in adoption practice to make two assumptions. The first was that as the baby was the product of the intrapsychic turmoil experienced by an emotionally disturbed woman, the child was not wanted for his or her own sake. The mother had the baby in order to meet her own needs and not those of the child. This was unlikely to make her a good mother. The second assumption which follows closely on the heels of the first is that the baby would be better off adopted:

> It is not an unwarranted interference with the unmarried mother to presume that in most cases it will be in the child's best interests for her to release her child for adoption ... The concept that the unmarried mother and her child constitute a family is to me unsupportable.
>
> (Reid, 1957, p.27, quoted in Roberts, ed., 1966, p.115)

The unmarried mother often found herself in a Catch 22 as far as her plans were concerned. The girl who relinquished her baby for adoption was deemed to be a mentally healthier woman than the one who did not. It was the mature thing to do. Of course, the girl only achieved this accolade of mental well-being if she was prepared to lose her baby. Keeping her baby was an immature act, and so a woman who did not surrender her baby was, *ipso facto*, immature and unfit to be a mother. In general, adoption workers practising in the 1940s and 1950s held explanatory models that justified what they were doing, making their world feel cosy and consistent. They were simply providing a more able set of parents for the children of unfit mothers who, in turn, would be much better off without the responsibility of bringing up a child at that particular moment in their lives. On the positive side, the psychiatric model attempted a more sympathetic view of the unwed mother's conduct, though the stigma of illegitimacy still surrounded the child and his or her birth.

CLASS, CHARACTER AND COMPETENCE

Vincent (1966) sought to explain the differential distribution of unmarried mothers between the social classes. He suggests that a society's values do not all pull in the same direction and that people are inconsistent in their attitudes towards certain classes of behaviour. So, for example, it need not be the case that a society both frowns on sexual relationships before marriage and condemns illegitimacy. Indeed, believes Vincent, modern Western societies have become increasingly permissive towards sexual relationships outside marriage but, until recently at least, they have remained bothered by and critical of births outside marriage. Roberts, writing in 1966, was worried that children born outside marriage were less likely to become competent members of society. The answer to the problem of the unmarried mother was not

> to look for a solution to the social problem of illegitimacy in a reform of social attitudes towards the unwed mother and her child. The best knowledge which we have available indicates that a complete family – composed of a sociological father and mother – is necessary to produce an adequately socialized adult ... if society were to encourage or tolerate illegitimacy it would be contributing to its demise.
>
> (Roberts, 1966, p.8)

It is clear that attitudes towards sexual behaviour can be confused and confusing. Tolerance and the promotion of sexual freedom on the one hand coupled with intolerance and the stigmatization of illegitimacy on the other create a recipe for producing more children born outside marriage without making it any easier for unmarried mothers to care for them. This leads to an increase in babies placed for adoption. Britain's peak year for adoptions was 1968. It was a time of increased sexual activity amongst the young, though the shame of unmarried motherhood remained strong. With the increasing number of illegitimate births at this time, it followed that there would be a rise in the number of babies placed for adoption. However, since 1968, society has gradually become more tolerant of the unmarried mother, though official support of her remains muted. As the number of babies born outside marriage continues to grow, so the number of babies placed for adoption has steadily fallen. It is the belief of Triseliotis (1989, p.23) that as a country's living conditions improve there is a corresponding reduction in the social stigma associated with births outside marriage. In developing this point, he suggests that there is a close relationship between poverty and the number of children available for adoption. Whereas illegitimacy and poverty lead to many poor women placing their babies for adoption, illegitimacy and affluence simply see a rise in the number of unmarried mothers, with only a few babies placed for adoption.

Thoughts about the unmarried mother and the adopted child undergo further refinements by Yelloly (1965). In her study of 160 women who had a baby outside marriage, 88 mothers kept their child while 72 decided to surrender the infant to adoption. Yelloly observed several differences between the mothers who kept their babies and those who did not. In particular, she noticed that women who decided to place their baby for adoption were much more likely to have parents who were strongly in favour of this option, whereas women who had parents who were willing to accept the child into the family were more prone to keep the baby. About a third of the mothers who placed their baby for adoption already had a child, compared to only 13 per cent of those who chose to keep their baby. One further factor seemed to influence a mother's predisposition to go for adoption. Whereas 43 per cent of those who chose adoption said that the child's putative father was married, this was true for only 24 per cent of those who kept their baby. In 82 per cent of the cases in which the child was adopted, at least one of the three characteristics – mother's parents were pro-adoption, previous child and married putative father – was present.

One of the works to which Yelloly refers is that carried out by Jones et al. (1966). These authors studied 113 women. Amongst their conclusions was that the unmarried mothers who kept their babies were likely to be insecure and anxious, tense and excitable, intellectually dull and immature. In contrast, mothers who surrendered their babies for adoption were found to be of greater intelligence, independence and emotional stability. They showed less anxiety and were less inclined to feel that other people made things difficult for them (also see Vincent, 1966). Over ten years later, Lightman and Schlesinger (1982) were producing similar results. Single mothers who placed their baby for adoption were more likely to be at school, living at home with parents who were usually very much involved with making plans for the baby, not in contact with the putative father and unlikely to have had a psychiatric history. In contrast, single mothers who kept their children had usually left school, had often left home, were more likely to have other unmarried mothers as friends and were three times more likely to have undergone psychiatric treatment in the past. Their parents were often divorced or separated and they were often in contact with the child's father.

In America, differences in adoption rates have been observed between the classes and the races, although it appears that race might be subsumed under class when it is appreciated that most blacks are also working class. Kronick (1966, p.249) observes that middle-class families are more prone to reject their unmarried daughter if she becomes pregnant, and certainly less likely to help her keep the child. In contrast, unmarried black women and working-class white women tend to keep their children. When education and religion are added, Kronick concludes that if the unmarried mother is young, educated and a non-Catholic, it is more likely that she will surrender her baby for adoption.

When considered together, these and other studies appeared to be telling us that the mothers least able to cope were most likely to keep their babies (Benet, 1976, p.177). But although the more socially and emotionally competent women were the most likely to place their child for adoption, we are left contemplating our thesis that the fate of unmarried mothers and their children is determined by the social climate in which they find themselves. That the more competent women chose not to raise their own children can be interpreted as further evidence of their ability to assess matters realistically. Their lives, without the baby, are generally going to be less complicated and less stressful, allowing them further opportunities to demonstrate their ability to cope and be competent. However, they have still lost their child. Adoption is an option because society has made it legally available and its legal availability in turn reflects the assumption that being an unmarried mother is unfortunate and certainly not a condition to be supported, never mind encouraged, and that children might be better reared by substitute parents who make no further reference to the birth mother.

The mothers who did keep their children faced many difficulties. Weir concluded her study of unmarried mothers saying that 'To these women, their babies represent the most important primary relationship they have' (1968, p.66). However, because of their own problems and family difficulties, coupled with the lack of support by state services, these women found it hard to be successful single parents. Adoption, therefore, has all the outward appearances of a reasonable solution to a difficult problem. But being an unmarried mother is a problem to the extent that society has defined it as a problem. By its failure to provide material, moral and emotional support, society has made the life of a single parent an arduous undertaking. Adoption is only to be viewed as a reasonable course of action under circumstances which may themselves be unreasonable. For example, Gill compares America with Denmark in 1969. In American society, where childbirth outside marriage was condemned and little moral or material support was provided for the single parent, the chances of the unmarried mother placing her child for adoption were high. Denmark, in contrast, offered the unmarried mother a good deal of help with housing, nursery places and money. In Denmark, the adoption rate of illegitimate children was only 2–3 per cent (Gill, 1977, p.105).

Two final thoughts are triggered by these studies. Over the years it has often been argued that illegitimate children who are adopted fare better in life than those who remain with their mothers (e.g. Seglow *et al.*, 1972). However, rather than interpret these findings as simple evidence which supports the superiority of adoption over retention, it might simply be that children who are not adopted remain with less stable and less able mothers. Were adopted children to have been kept by their comparatively more able and competent unmarried mothers, they might have developed at least as well as they did as adopted children. In contrast, if that same mother, previously unmarried, marries and has a further child, the arguments about her fitness to be a mother shift, if not disappear altogether. Coming from the opposite direction, Macintyre (1977, p.160) makes the same point: 'At ᵔits crudest, the account "I gave my child away for its own good" may not be acceptable from married women, but be exceedingly acceptable from unmarried women.' The cultural context in which the unmarried mother finds herself and the attitudes towards having children outside marriage play a major part in determining whether or not she keeps her child.

THE SOCIAL CHARACTER OF ADOPTION

Echoes of the psychiatric model are still heard today, though even in its heyday doubts were being expressed. In 1954, Vincent pointed out that many studies of the unmarried mother took their samples from public institutions, welfare agencies and psychiatric clinics. The researchers were simply dealing with a biased group of unmarried mothers who were in contact with the agency because of their emotionally unstable condition. So, in spite of the 'treatment' regimes promoted by psychiatric theorists, illegitimacy continued. It was also noticed that the social and geographical distribution of unmarried mothers was not uniform. This cast further doubt on the idea that the unwed mother was simply a girl who was emotionally disturbed and instead revived theories that were based on the cultural and social experience of the mother. This brings us back to the view that the adoption of illegitimate children and the way the unmarried mother experiences this event is a product of her society's attitudes towards and explanations of illegitimacy and the 'giving up' of children.

One of the most eloquent arguments along these lines is offered by Mary Kathleen Benet in her book *The Character of Adoption*, written in 1976. Social situations that contain a mixture of sexuality, family life and matters of kinship are bound to produce strong and powerful feelings. Adoption has been attacked as a practice that encourages promiscuity because it allows unmarried women to 'get away' with the consequences of their immoral behaviour. It has also been condemned as an activity that allows rich, middle-class, childless couples to appropriate the children of the poor. All the fancy psychological theorizing to justify the practice is no more than an excuse to transfer the children of the weak and disadvantaged to the strong and prosperous. Benet reminds us, though, that different cultures handle strong and powerful feelings, as well as illegitimacy and adoption, in different ways.

In the modern West, adoption was seen as the rescue of a child from a disadvantaged and even harmful parent. The ideal was to sever all links between the child's past and his or her present adoptive family. The transfer of parental roles was made more and more secure and complete. Birth parents and adopters should remain unknown to one another. Secrecy was to surround the adoption process. This practice is emotionally tough and austere. Modern societies are formed so that both adults and children meet most of their emotional needs and establish long-term relationships only within the nuclear family. 'Hence,' writes Tizard (1977, p.2), 'couples without children, and children without parents, are likely to have unsatisfied needs for giving and receiving affection, and for maintaining relationships.'

> This emphasis on the nuclear family means that the few remaining ties – those between husband and wife, parents and children – are closer and more intense than ever before. The tribe member can surrender his children with comparative equanimity, knowing that the separation is not complete and that he in turn will receive other children to foster. But to the modern parent, relinquishing a child for adoption deprives him of one of his only human contacts. Thus the only children who are given up for adoption are those whose own parents are really unable to keep them – either because of the opprobrium attached to unmarried parenthood or because of poverty, extreme youth and other practical handicaps.
>
> (Benet, 1976, p.15)

Underlying Western adoption practices has been the belief that it is second best and ideally 'not supposed' to happen. But Benet provocatively compares our own models of adoption with what has been practised in the ancient past and what is practised in the non-Western present. She discovers that in many societies, not only is adoption viewed more openly, it is often 'supposed' to happen. African, Caribbean, Indian, Polynesian and Eskimo communities appear to practise kinship fostering and outright adoption to a much greater extent than has been the case in white Western societies. However, children are not irretrievably lost to mothers or fathers, even though they may be raised by aunts and uncles, grandparents or neighbours. They are shared and become part of the community's population of children. Not only does this take much of the intensity away from parent–child relationships experienced in the isolated nuclear family, it encourages a communal responsibility for the next generation. Benet (ibid., p.17) sees adoption in these groups as a means of strengthening the extended family and integrating people into their community by weakening the exclusive bond between parents and children. All of which is in marked contrast to the rupturing and disintegration of relationships that characterizes life in the industrialized, urban West. Benet explains Western practices by returning us to the changes already under way in medieval England. 'If adoption is to exist at all in a society where possession, ownership and materialism hold sway it must be made absolutely total and watertight' (ibid., p.79). If a child is adopted, the birth parents are generally required to surrender all legal claims to the child. They are required to disappear from the child's future development. For example, in many states in America it was thought good practice to erase the stigma of illegitimacy for the child's own well-being. Upon adoption the child was issued with an amended birth certificate giving him or her the name of the adoptive parents, providing a symbolic break from the birth mother. Typically, original birth certificates were sealed and made available only with a court order. 'When in many jurisdictions the original parent's name was removed also from the adoption decree, adoption had become institutionally invisible. If the intent of the law and policy was to make it indistinguishable from its consanguine counterpart, the adoptive family had virtually succeeded in its mimicry' (Kirk and McDaniel, 1984, pp.76–7). The birth mother loses all her rights to the child. We have the curious position in which adoption practices value biological birth and parenting so much that they seek to be as much like them as possible, while at the same time such practices endeavour to exclude the birth mother from the child's subsequent upbringing. This practice has received a good deal of scientific backing over the years and it is only recently that evidence has been mustered to suggest that such an absolutist and exclusive attitude to adoption may not necessarily offer the child the best developmental prospects. The ideas of people like Benet upset any cosy notions that adoption is a neat solution to the problems experienced by birth mothers, illegitimate children and childless couples. If having a child as an unmarried woman is not a problem and if mothers can retain open and relaxed access to children whom they have placed with other parents, then the stresses and strains surrounding unmarried motherhood and relinquishment disappear.

These cultural and historical comparisons drive home the point that the way a community handles illegitimacy and adoption profoundly affects the experience of being an unmarried mother and the relinquishment of children for adoption. Unmarried mothers might therefore experience a range of social reactions. Having children outside marriage might be seen as normal, unremarkable and manageable, so that mothers are able to keep their children or at least 'share' them, thus making adoption unnecessary. This appears to be the trend in this country, with an increasing proportion of babies born to unmarried mothers and yet fewer babies than ever available for adoption. Another variation might be that children, whether born inside or outside marriage, are the concern of the extended family and indeed the whole community and so adoption (or kinship fostering) is seen as normal. The child is not lost to his or her parents and the mother experiences no feelings of loss or guilt. But the more condemning people are of sexual relations outside marriage, the more guilty, upset and angry will those who have been discovered to be in such relationships feel. And if the unmarried woman has a child, her ability to keep that child will be determined by the provisions made by her society to support single parents. If the child is to be cared for by others, the mother may experience this as a profound loss, as all links are severed between her and her baby. Thus piled one upon the other are a series of difficult, painful and shameful experiences for the unmarried mother who is constrained to place her baby for adoption by a society that does not make it easy for her to keep the child.

LOSE EVERY WHICH WAY

Our contention throughout this opening chapter has been that the unmarried mother's experience of pregnancy, birth and single parenthood is constructed by the ideas and attitudes that people have towards women who have sex and children outside marriage.

Once an unmarried woman finds herself with a baby and no supportive partner or parents, she will be on the receiving end of a series of moral pronouncements: having a baby without being married is wrong; keeping a baby without being married is wrong; failing your children by giving them away is unmotherly and unwomanly and therefore wrong. By obeying one moral injunction the unmarried mother will inevitably fall foul of another. In breaching moral codes, social norms, family standards and measures of psychological maturity, the birth mother experiences a depressing cocktail of feelings of shame, guilt, failure and inadequacy.

Her difficulties do not stop there. Compounding her dilemma, she will experience further problems whether she decides to keep the child or not. If she chooses to look after the baby herself, little in the way of support will be offered. As a single parent, her life will be a struggle. Her career prospects will be reduced. She may learn that the children of single parents are disadvantaged in many ways. If she relinquishes her baby for adoption, she will experience all the emotions and pain associated with a profound loss. Adoption practice generally demands complete severance of all links between the birth mother and her child, thus making the loss a socially contrived event rather than a naturally imposed one. The unmarried mother who chooses adoption will find herself at the end of a process that will have made her the subject of a variety of social, moral and psychological definitions, almost always unflattering. Her position is not only unenviable but also a source of major psychological stress.

The important point to emphasize is that there is nothing inherently stressful in having a baby as an unmarried mother other than the usual feelings of any woman having a child. All that she experiences is a product of the social, moral and theoretical climates that surround her behaviour, including any expectations held by her society that illegitimate babies should be adopted and, if adopted, on whether or not the birth mother should remain in contact with her child. Change the climate and you change the experience. Following this line of thought, we do not need to explain the birth mother as a birth mother, for in a sense there is nothing to explain. But in order to understand what it feels like to be a birth mother we do have to understand how she is explained and treated, for it is in these explanations and treatments that she comes to define, understand and experience herself. What she thinks and feels, what she can do and believes she should do, are composed within the ideas that inform her society's attitude to the unmarried mother and her child.

2

Understanding the Birth Mother

MORAL LUCK

In choosing to understand the birth mother rather than explain her, we still need to consider the circumstances that give rise to her dilemma. The curious concept of 'moral luck' will help us. It is an intriguing notion spawned by philosophers who had a strong suspicion that not only do people experience luck, either good or bad, but they are then judged in the light of that luck.

For example, consider two drunken drivers. On his way home one careers on to the pavement and back on to the road, but in the process his car hits a pedestrian, who is run over and killed. Manslaughter receives a harsh judgement and the punishment is severe. Another drunken driver wandering equally dangerously over the road is lucky and does not bump into anyone. He is judged merely careless and punished relatively lightly. Although the behaviour of the second motorist is equally reckless, he is treated in a more lenient manner. Nagel (1979, p.29) offers another example. The penalty for attempted murder is less than that for successful murder, even though both assailants intended to take the life of another person. Culpability, it seems, can depend on such things as whether the victim happened to be wearing a bulletproof vest, or whether a bird flew into the path of the bullet, matters beyond the control of the would-be murderer.

What moral luck amounts to is that some actions are judged and treated in the light of *how things turned out* and not in terms of what their author intended. We usually imagine that a person's moral vigour is judged by investigating his or her motives in pursuing a course of action, but with moral luck the ethical examination works in reverse. We decide on a person's moral status by considering the consequences of their actions. Although on the face of it this produces a very queer ethics, in practice people are often judged by how things turned out rather than on what they intended.

In the case of birth mothers, first let us concede that the majority of unmarried women have sexual intercourse. Through bad luck, some of these women will become pregnant and have babies, so becoming unmarried mothers. This is Pauker's empirical conclusion. Chance, he believes, is the likely explanation of most teenage pregnancies: 'out-of-wedlock babies are the result of neither the stork nor a desire for an out-of-wedlock child but rather the result of sexual intercourse' (Pauker, 1969, p.66). Unmarried mothers are judged, often unsympathetically, in terms of the way things turned out (they had a child out of wedlock) and not in terms of their original motives (to have sexual relations with a man). The women who did not get pregnant and yet entertained exactly the same intentions find that their moral standing remains in a reasonably sound state. In contrast, the women who had a baby through a piece of bad luck find that all aspects of their lives, their morals and their character are reassessed, not in terms of the intentions shared with all other sexually active young women, but solely in terms of the unintended outcome. The unmarried mother's alleged moral condition derives entirely from her bad luck. However, once the mother is ascribed a moral condition, some people feel that her behaviour is then available for clinical explanation. They believe that there must be reasons (either conscious or unconscious) for the woman wanting a baby. The outcome is taken as evidence that there was a deliberate intention for which an explanation might be sought. Once her condition is defined, the definition determines the way she is treated, the way she experiences that treatment and the way she views herself.

A variation on this theme is explored by Macintyre (1977). She compares the fortunes of married mothers and unmarried mothers. All the assumptions about what is normal, healthy, natural, feminine, instinctive and wonderful for married women are different for women who happen not to be married. She summarizes the double-think in this fashion:

FOR MARRIED WOMEN

1. Pregnancy and childbearing are normal and desirable, and conversely a desire not to have at least some children aberrant and in need of explanation.

2. Pregnancy and childbearing are not problematic and for a woman to treat them as such indicates that she is not normal.
3. Legitimate children with a living parent should not be surrendered for adoption or taken from the mother.
4. The loss of a baby by miscarriage, stillbirth or neonatal death will occasion deep, instinctive distress and grief.

FOR SINGLE WOMEN

1. Pregnancy and childbearing are abnormal and undesirable, and the desire to have a baby is aberrant, selfish and in need of explanation.
2. Pregnancy and childbearing are problematic and for a woman not to treat them as such indicates that she is not normal.
3. It is usually best for an illegitimate child of a single mother to be surrendered for adoption, and a woman who wishes to keep her baby is unrealistic and selfish.
4. The loss of a baby by miscarriage, stillbirth or neonatal death should not occasion too much distress or grief, and may produce relief.

IN SUMMARY

One solution to the 'problems' of the single pregnant woman is to get married. If she is going to get married she will want the baby; if not, she will not.

(Macintyre, 1977, p.184)

Adoption practice reflects the belief that all mothers and their children should, in some way, be attached to a man, preferably the child's father and the woman's husband. If a woman cannot provide herself and her child with such a man, then the next best thing is for the child to be adopted by a woman who does have such a man. Inglis, however, writes that 'the surrender of a child by a mother to strangers is abnormal' (1984, p.ix). The separation is 'part of an idealized and fiercely guarded social system involving the expectation that all girls be virtuous, all women be mothers and all mothers be wives' (ibid., pp.x–xi).

With the ideas of Chapter 1 still clearly in mind, we need to remind ourselves that many of the experiences of the unmarried mother, particularly those who have had a child adopted, are a direct result of the way she is regarded by friends and relatives, professionals and politicians. The circumstances and reactions that give rise to her experience of being a birth mother are manufactured by the people around her. To a large extent, what she thinks and feels about being a birth mother is socially constructed and not a natural feature of being an unmarried woman who places her child for adoption. The feelings of distress and being at fault are soon followed by those of shame and guilt. The net result of so many moral strictures adds to the normal stresses and strains experienced by any woman having a baby. All things considered – the shock of finding yourself pregnant, the reactions of family and friends, the disruption to career and education, the realization that major decisions about the baby have to be made – it is no surprise to learn that becoming an unmarried mother is a very stressful thing. The stress level is maintained after the baby is born, whether the mother decides to keep the child or not. But for those who choose to relinquish their child, a new ingredient enters their psychological turmoil – loss. Stress and loss are the two major experiences that beset most women who decide that their baby has to be adopted.

Without question, our understanding of the birth mother has been increased greatly by the pioneering work of Robin Winkler and Margaret van Keppel (1984). Their studies of the long-term adjustment of mothers who relinquish a child for adoption provide a number of valuable insights that help us understand the birth mother and the feelings with which she has to live. The rest of this chapter takes advantage of their work.

In an Australian national study of 213 unmarried, unpartnered women who had relinquished a first child for adoption, Winkler and van Keppel (1984) sought to answer two questions:

1. What are the effects of relinquishment on the mother who places her child for adoption?
2. What factors make adjustment to relinquishment more and less difficult?

Most of the mothers in the study said that they relinquished their child because they were single and poor or because they felt they were too young and under pressure from parents. After a thorough review of what others before them had thought and said, the researchers developed a theoretical framework based on two themes: relinquishment as loss and relinquishment as a stressful life-event. It was clear from the earlier works that birth mothers suffered feelings that were both confusing and complex. Many mothers continued to mourn the loss of their child for years afterwards, some even finding that their pain intensified with time. Feelings of regret and guilt were experienced by others. The majority of birth mothers wanted to know how their child was growing up, and many thought that one day they would like to meet their son or daughter.

To help give their ideas some shape, Winkler and van Keppel make a telling comparison with mothers who suffer a perinatal death – mothers who lose their baby at birth or sometime during the first week of life. It emerges that women who lose a baby through adoption have many experiences in common with those who lose a baby through death. A well-understood sequence of reactions follows a major loss, whether that loss be of a relationship (through death or divorce) or a limb (by amputation or accident) or a job (because of retirement or redundancy) or a baby (by adoption or death). Over a period of time the person suffering the loss might be expected to go through the following grief reactions: shock and disbelief, anger and resentment, guilt, depression and withdrawal, before finally reaching a stage of acceptance and resolution. This sequence of grief reactions is entirely normal.

However, it is also recognized that a person's ability to negotiate each stage of the grief reaction is affected by the behaviour and attitude of other people. What people say and don't say, what people do and don't do, profoundly affects the way someone copes with a loss. If relatives or friends are thoughtless or insensitive, the grieving person may become stuck at some stage of the normal grieving process.

Several features conspire to make grieving particularly difficult for mothers whose babies die at or around the time of birth. The stillborn or dead baby may be quickly removed from the mother. She may have had no opportunity of holding her infant. Many mothers, though not all, say that they find that their ability to grieve is easier if they have had a chance to hold as well as see their dead baby. During pregnancy, the baby becomes part of the mother so that when the child dies she feels she has lost a part of herself. It is common for mothers in this situation to feel that they have failed as a woman. They have failed to bring a live child into the world and feel some degree of responsibility for the death. These feelings generate questions such as 'What did I do in the pregnancy to cause this?', 'What didn't I do?', 'What am I being punished for?' (Helmrath and Steinitz, 1978, p.787). Both shame and guilt may be experienced.

Relatives and hospital staff may promote a 'conspiracy of silence'. No one talks about the baby or the death. The mother is not encouraged to express her feelings. People carry on as if nothing of fundamental import has happened. A sense of isolation is suffered. Other people expect the mother to 'put the death behind her and get on with her life'. 'In all cases,' reported Helmrath and Steinitz, 'the couples began to feel that they were behaving inappropriately because they were grieving, rather than realizing that it was the external system that was inappropriate. With no acknowledgement of the infant's existence, keeping the baby real became a major task' (ibid., p.788). Family and friends failed to experience the baby as a known, familiar individual. They formed no attachment to the infant. They also failed to recognize that the mother *had* become attached to her baby. This might explain why family and friends gave little effective support to the mother, had no need to talk about the dead child, and, in effect, suppressed the mother's ability to grieve.

The parallels with the mother who loses her baby by adoption are striking (Winkler and van Keppel, 1984, pp.9–10):

1. The baby is often removed from the mother straight after birth. Though less common today, in the past many mothers would not be allowed to see their baby.
2. It is not unusual for doctors, midwives and social workers to discourage mothers from forming a relationship with their baby. Again, many mothers report that they feel as if they have lost a part of themselves.
3. As well as hospital staff and relatives, adoption workers and friends sponsor a 'conspiracy of silence', believing that it is

best for the mother to forget about the whole episode and try, as quickly as possible, to make a fresh start in life.

But for the mother who loses her baby by adoption, Winkler and van Keppel and others recognize three additional factors peculiar to adoption. These extra dimensions further disturb and distort the birth mother's ability to grieve:

4. There is the shame and guilt of having had a sexual relationship outside marriage. There is also the shame and guilt associated with failing as a mother. Having got pregnant under morally censured circumstances, the unmarried mother compounds her 'crime' by not bringing up her own child. A climate of punishment and censure often seems to surround the mother who surrenders her baby for adoption.

5. Like the mother who suffers a perinatal death, the birth mother also feels responsible for what has happened, but to a much greater degree – her loss is self-inflicted.

6. In spite of the loss, the child continues to exist, although adoption practice generally denies the mother any knowledge about the progress and welfare of her child. The child's continued existence confuses the grieving process.

Winkler and van Keppel found that about half of the women who relinquished a child for adoption adjusted reasonably well to their loss; they suffered no long-term adverse effects. The remaining half adjusted less well, many experiencing pain and distress years later. It is important not to lose sight of the women who did manage to make a good recovery once the baby was adopted. By listening to their experiences we can learn what factors helped them make a good adjustment to the loss of their baby. We shall highlight three of the most important findings.

The first establishes that *relinquishment is a stressful life-event.* Over half of the women said that having a child adopted was the most stressful thing they had ever experienced, many adding that the effects were still with them years later. The remainder said that it compared with other stressful events including such things as the death of a child or a divorce.

The second finding reports that, on average, *women who lose a baby by adoption show a greater degree of psychological impairment* than those of a matched sample of women whose babies were not adopted. This means that birth mothers are more liable than other unmarried mothers to suffer depression, anxiety, alcohol abuse and physical ill health (also see Burnell and Norfleet, 1979). There is even the suspicion of secondary infertility – that birth mothers who want further children are less able to conceive than other women who wish for second children (Deykin *et al.*, 1984, p.276). Half of the mothers experienced a persistent and increasing sense of loss over periods of up to thirty years.

The third result shows that *successful adjustment is possible* and that there are identifiable elements in the birth mother's environment which help her adjust to the experience of loss. These include social support and the opportunity to express feelings and her sense of loss.

Birth mothers who felt that family and friends were understanding and supportive made better adjustments to their loss. Support requires that people are not just available and around, but that when needed they are able to listen in a sympathetic and understanding manner. The grieving person should feel wanted, valued and cared for, their feelings should be acknowledged and accepted. One mother recalled, 'I don't have any feelings of guilt or regret, and I think I owe that mainly to my parents who stood by me the whole time and gave me their love and support' (Winkler and van Keppel, 1984, p.46). Although the first twelve months are the most important time for good support, things turn out even more happily if this support is maintained beyond the one-year period. The relinquished child continues to exist and this protracts the time needed to adjust. 'As the years pass and the mother grows older and knows the child may have grown up, the need to know the lost child becomes pressing in a new way. Relinquishment is a particularly lingering process' (ibid., p.62).

A need to talk openly and express feelings about the lost child was reported by most birth mothers. For the majority, however, the need remained unmet. 'Every time I tried to talk,' recollected a birth mother, 'I was told that it was all in the past, my life had begun again. I was more confused than ever when no one would let me talk' (Deykin *et al.*, 1984, p.49). In most cases the 'conspiracy of silence' was maintained, implicitly encouraging birth mothers to deny their fertility and to forget their adopted child. Van Keppel (1986, p.2) goes on to remind us that many people argue that the 'conspiracy of silence' is a thoughtful practice, one which allows the birth mother to preserve her honour. And there are yet others who believe that because the child was given away for adoption, the mother probably did not care about the child, which is why talking with her would be a waste of time. And yet, in truth, the birth mother's need to talk and express her feelings continues well beyond the first year, as the following quote shows: 'When I was about to marry my husband I told him about my child – he forbade me to ever mention him again. I have had to keep all my feelings to myself and it hurts like hell at times' (Winkler and van Keppel, 1984, p.49). 'They suffer in silence,' writes van Keppel (1986, p.5), 'because of a belief that theirs is an abnormal reaction and that they are somehow more disturbed than their decision has warranted.' It was quite clear to the researchers that opportunities for the birth mother to express her feelings helped her to make a better adjustment.

Those birth mothers who did not adjust well to their relinquishment continued to feel a strong sense of loss. Nearly half of the mothers in the study said that their sense of loss had intensified over the years, leaving 38 per cent who reported that it had weakened, 12 per cent who said it had disappeared, and 6 per cent who felt that it had remained the same (Winkler and van Keppel, 1984, p.67). The sense of loss varied over time, but tended to be most acute around the child's birthday, when the child started school or reached eighteen, and when the birth mother had more children of her own. Such feelings of loss were aggravated by the legal restrictions surrounding adoption practice. It seemed apparent that the birth mother's continued sense of loss and weakened ability to adjust were in part related to her lack of knowledge about the child's development, her inability to let the child know that she still cared and thought about him or her, and the thin hope that one day she might meet her son or daughter. That the child continued to exist and was growing up without her, and forbidden as she was to know anything about what was happening, meant that her ability to grieve in any normal fashion was greatly impaired.

THE BIRTH MOTHER'S EXPERIENCE:
TELLING HER STORY

What do we know about the one in twenty-five women who have given up a child for adoption? Who are these birth mothers? It is, in fact, quite hard to provide detailed answers to questions such as these. All we do know is that at the time they became pregnant these women were likely to be young, unmarried and living at home with their parents.

Prior to the late 1970s, those who studied women who gave up a child for adoption tended to do one of two things. They either *described* the birth mother in terms of her age, background and personality, or they *explained* her in terms of her psychology, exploring the reasons why she became pregnant but then surrendered the baby for adoption. However, there were some who wanted to change the style of inquiry. Dissatisfactions were felt about the dry, somewhat lifeless picture of the birth mother that was drawn in surveys and theories of the unwed mother. Rather than employ an expert to describe and explain the birth mother objectively, the thing to do was to seek the birth mother's own subjective view of what had happened to her. In short, she was invited to 'tell her story'. The traditional methods of social research had failed to hear what the birth mother was saying.

> As we have listened for centuries to the voices of men ... so we have come more recently to notice not only the silence of women but the difficulty of hearing what they say when they speak ... the failure to see the reality of women's lives and to hear the differences in their voices stems in part from the mode of social experience and interpretation.
>
> (Gilligan, 1982, pp.173-4)

The best examples of birth mothers beginning to tell their stories are to be found in Joss Shawyer's book *Death by Adoption*, published in 1979, and *Living Mistakes: Mothers Who Consented to Adoption* by Kate Inglis, published in 1984. Although not as detailed, many of the letters reported in *The Adoption Triangle*, by Sorosky *et al.* (1978), also give a strong flavour of how the world looks from the point of view of the birth mother. In contrast to the analytical and clinical studies of earlier years, the 'stories' have a powerful and immediate impact on the emotions of the reader. You are drawn rapidly into the turbulent world of women who suddenly find themselves having to cope with huge, often overwhelming changes in their lives. Reich (1988, p.2) observes that in many of the stories there is a 'subtext' which explores the imbalance of power between the strong and privileged and the weak and disadvantaged. 'The most vulnerable and helpless figure in the story, even if only by omission, is usually the original mother.' What these innovative texts do is give the birth mother a voice so that she can be heard by a world which is inclined to forget or deny her existence. And once her voice has been heard, adoption loses its sweet innocence. It can no longer claim to be the neat, simple solution to everyone's problem. There is a price, sometimes a heavy price, to be paid.

The emergence of the birth mother and her view has been gradual and is not yet complete. For example, although we know that many black children have been adopted by white families, the black mother has not yet spoken, and in spite of our best efforts, her voice remains largely unheard. For years, decency had demanded that the birth mother remain silent and socially invisible. However, we now appreciate enough of her experience to realize that she is not someone who should be expected to bow out of the adoption story gracefully, keeping her silence for the sake of the child and the adoptive parents. Her needs must be recognized. The feelings she has for her lost child have to be valued. The psychological impact of relinquishing a baby for adoption must be understood. And although for years the wisdom has been that once the child has been placed with adopters the birth mother should quietly disappear and not speak, doubts are now cast about such a wisdom. She should remain a real person for the adopted child, a person who, like the child, continues to grow and change. There are strong suspicions that the emotional health of all those involved in the adoption triangle is better served not by banishing the birth mother from the story but by allowing her to remain a real person who, in many cases, retains a real interest in the progress and development of her child.

REACTIONS AND RELATIONSHIPS

It is our basic contention that the meaning which the birth mother gives to her experiences is forged in the relationships that she has with those around her as they react to what is happening. In general, it appears that the reactions of people to the unwed mother not only create feelings of stress, trauma and shame in the mother-to-be, but those same reactions lead her to conclude that adoption is the only way out of her increasingly complex situation. Then, having made such a difficult decision, she finds that no one appears to show much understanding of the enormity of what she has done. In spite of the strength and integrity that informed her decision, her moral standing remains of a low order. Indeed, in many subtle and not so subtle ways she is further diminished; she has now failed both as a virtuous woman and as a successful mother.

The mother is acutely aware of how the world is viewing her and it is within this highly charged emotional arena that she works out the meaning of what she has done (become pregnant as an unmarried woman), what she must do (relinquish the baby, forget all about the unfortunate episode and make a fresh start), and what kind of woman she is (one who has had sex and a child outside marriage and who gives that child away). When we hear the birth mother telling her story, the account she gives takes on its particular content, form and emotional intensity as she reacts and responds to the important people in her life at the time.

Listening to birth mothers speak of their experiences, there is a remarkable similarity and consistency in what they say and feel. All birth mothers are on the receiving end of other people's strong and opinionated views about sex and pregnancy outside marriage. It is the reaction of these other people which turns pregnancy, birth and motherhood into a series of 'stressful life-events'.

Over the next three chapters we shall trace the themes that run through the birth mothers' stories. We shall see that each theme is defined along two dimensions: certain people and particular events. The way certain people react to particular events produces the themes common to the experience of being a birth mother. Three events or phases in the birth mother's life can be distinguished: (i) the pregnancy, (ii) the baby's birth and adoption and (iii) her life as a woman who gave up a child for adoption.

The works of Sorosky *et al.* (1978), Shawyer (1979) and Inglis (1984) have already been mentioned and we shall be making use of their spirited reporting. To these three pioneer texts, we need to add the more recent accounts given by Jenny Rockel and Murray Ryburn in their book *Adoption Today*, published in 1988. The final thread in this weave comes from our own work with birth mothers. We, too, have stories to tell on behalf of mothers who gave up their child for adoption. Quotes which are not attributed to a particular author arise out of our own work with birth mothers. Along with the other authors, we wish to preserve the birth mothers' anonymity and so, like them, wherever necessary we have changed names and disguised details.

3
The Unwed and the Unborn

From the moment she discovers that she is pregnant the life of the birth mother is never to be the same again. Her pregnancy is a time of emotional, physical and social turmoil in which the mother-to-be finds her world turned upside down and inside out. She is having an unplanned baby at a disastrously inconvenient time, under hopelessly inappropriate conditions and by a man whom she might not love or even like. Whatever she had in mind by way of a career or education has to be radically rethought or abandoned. Often she has to leave home, change towns and encounter new people at short notice. She may be young and inexperienced in the ways of the world and in no way does she feel prepared to face the huge changes that are about to overtake her life.

Being pregnant involves coping with the reactions of many other people. In following the birth mother's story, we shall start by listening to what she felt herself when she first learned that she was pregnant. For most women, the next task is to tell their parents. Their reaction is critical in determining the way the pregnancy is handled and experienced. The man who got her pregnant appears less important, at least in terms of what the mother thinks and can do. Some of the men never even learned that they were the father of the baby. And beyond the birth mother's family and her relationship with the baby's father lie friends and neighbours, teachers and doctors, social workers and the women who run homes for unmarried mothers. These people, too, inform the climate in which the birth mother proceeds with her pregnancy.

THE UNMARRIED MOTHER-TO-BE

Upon learning that she is pregnant the birth mother is tossed along a series of emotional rapids that start with feelings of disbelief and dismay and often end with feelings of despair and dejection as the full impact of what is happening dawns upon her. Her feelings about the baby are usually mixed, but this is hardly surprising, as she is simultaneously buffeted by changes to her body, her moods, her social world and her physical environment. Becoming a mother can be both exciting and frightening. Thoughts of keeping the baby are as compelling as they are hopeless, while feelings about relinquishing the child can soothe just as easily as they can hurt.

Shock and Disbelief

In many instances the birth mother initially refused to believe that she could possibly be pregnant. 'I tried to deny it to myself,' remembered one mother. 'I'd wake up in the middle of the night and think "It's not really happening", and think "It'll be all right tomorrow" . . . I'd be getting up at four in the morning so I could be sick before my parents woke up, and I was pretending the sickness was because I was worried about my period, not because I was pregnant' (Rockel and Ryburn, 1988, p.23). Christine, who felt that she did not have the confidence at fifteen to say no to her boyfriend's insistence on having sex, found herself pregnant after the very first time she had had intercourse:

Anyway, we ended up having sex. It was quite a sordid affair. I had had no sex whatsoever. I lost my virginity. We changed the sheets afterwards. I helped him change the bed because there was a lot of blood . . . Then I didn't have my periods but I didn't accept that I could possibly be pregnant. I mean I thought it was the first time and he used a Durex so I can't be. I convinced myself that I was not, and my mother was making such a fuss about Moira, my sister, being pregnant that there was no way my mind could accept that I could be, so I just kept it totally hidden.

However, once it became impossible to continue denying the pregnancy, most birth mothers found themselves upset and shocked, as well as scared and frightened. Many found themselves in a mounting state of panic as the weeks went by and they still had not menstruated. Janet was eighteen and a nurse; it was the 1960s:

I realized very soon I was pregnant and that there was absolutely no relationship between me and the father. I did not, and still don't, feel any sense of resentment against him. I mean he was a fairly innocent sort of party. Well, first of all I thought I'd get rid of it, the baby, and somebody gave me some tablets which didn't work and it was pre the Abortion Act, and I think I was just messing about, and probably they were all totally ineffectual like taking Smarties. But after about six weeks or so I thought this baby is here to stay. I was on night duty and I was getting more and more depressed and upset and not sleeping during the day. I was very ill in the night and got taken to the medical centre, and I think I wasn't really ill at all, I think it was just a vehicle by which I could actually tell someone.

The combination of disbelief followed by shock led some mothers to resent and even hate the baby that was firmly lodged inside them, growing inexorably as a reminder of what they had done and how their lives were to change as a consequence. However, the mothers who harboured the strongest feelings of hatred for the baby, at least initially, were those who felt they had been cheated or sexually violated by the man who was the father of the child:

I thought the father didn't care. My mother said he denied the baby. I just did not want the child. I just wanted to get rid of it. I hated this thing in my body. I just felt that I didn't want this child whatever.

Fiona (Inglis, 1984) had been raped and sexually abused repeatedly by her stepfather from the age of fourteen. She was too scared to tell anyone and she could not be certain that her mother would believe her. When she was fifteen Fiona started missing her periods but dared not think that she might be pregnant. Her mother then announced that she herself was pregnant and Fiona felt horrified and sickened. She loathed and detested her stepfather. Day by day she felt herself getting fatter but she continued to ignore the possibility that she might be having a baby. She stayed in her room a lot, started talking to herself and did not hear what other people were saying. 'Everything felt out of control.' Eventually, the pregnancy was confirmed and Fiona's mother was upset, while her stepfather shouted that she was a 'little whore' and that she must have been 'sleeping around'. Fiona thought about killing herself and murdering her stepfather. But as time went by:

> I got fond of my baby; it was there all the time. I used to split off from what had happened and make up fantasies about a Big Romance and the boy getting killed in a car crash just before we were to marry . . . As long as I kept my stepfather out of my mind I loved my baby but felt absolute terror and horror when I let myself remember what had happened and how the baby got there. I would hate the baby then and felt it as a kind of poisonous lump growing in me.
>
> (ibid., pp.138–9)

One step even further down the road of sexual abuse was Louise (Shawyer, 1979). She was brought up in a very strict Reformed Seventh Day Adventist family. But since she had been a young girl her father had forced her to have sex with him. Her mother, who was very passive, said nothing. Louise did once complain to the Church but they said she was telling lies and that she must be sick. Not long after leaving home Louise became pregnant by another man, but because of her own sexual abuse the whole idea of having a baby was repugnant to her:

> The baby was just a horrible, dirty thing inside me, a very immoral thing. It wasn't a human being, a baby or anything, it was just a filthy horrible thing.
>
> (ibid., p.160)

However, at the other end of the spectrum were a few birth mothers who were not surprised at finding themselves pregnant and even felt pleased about their condition. Cassie, who was adopted herself, felt that her pregnancy was inevitable. 'I don't know this for sure but I suspect I was trying in some way to understand what had happened to my mother and me by going through it myself . . . I think that's where the story began; that I myself was adopted' (Inglis, 1984, p.147). When she did become pregnant Cassie 'was so excited, I was really so very happy and the reason, although I couldn't articulate it at the time, was this was the first time in my whole life there would be someone to whom I was blood-related' (ibid., p.152).

Shame and Guilt

Once the pregnancy was confirmed and the birth mother began to feel her body changing, many experienced feelings of shame. Their problem was one of how to cope with their new role and what it represented. In Goffman's splendid phrase, these women now found themselves having to manage a 'spoiled identity'. They carried a social stigma and as individuals they were now disqualified from full social acceptance. Goffman (1963) continues his discussion, observing that stigmas cause us to re-evaluate a person's moral worth. He makes a distinction between stigmas which are immediately visible (physical blemishes, abnormalities and differences) and those which are not (character aberrations and moral deficiencies). 'In the first case one deals with the *discredited*, in the second with that of the *discreditable*.' This is a useful distinction for our purposes. Whereas the obviously pregnant unmarried woman is morally discredited, the mother who has given up her child for adoption has an identity which is discreditable. In the latter case, although there are no visible indications that she is a morally flawed character, there is always the possibility that her 'true identity' will be discovered. She has the problem of 'information management' – how does the birth mother control what other people know about her? In contrast, the pregnant unmarried woman is less able to control what others know about her – she is plainly about to have a baby. Her problem is how to conduct herself as a morally discredited person.

Thus birth mothers have the problem of managing a spoiled identity at two stages in their lives. This affects the way they handle and experience all their social encounters. We shall return to the mother who has actually relinquished her child in Chapter 5, but meanwhile we need to stay with the unmarried woman who is recognizably pregnant. One of her first feelings is that of shame, knowing that she has breached both moral and social codes:

The shame was probably the biggest factor at the time – it was just overwhelming. It was something to do with the fact that it was obvious that I had had sex. And I was young, and I shouldn't have been having sex, and here was this big protruding stomach telling the world. And they could all point at me and say 'Shameful hussy!'

(Rockel and Ryburn, 1988, p.23)

Close on the heels of shame follows guilt, knowing that what you have done is wrong as well as a disgrace. Guilt was greatest in those women who came from homes in which there was a strong sense of the family's standing in the local social and moral order. Middle-class families whose social standing was threatened by the scandal of a pregnancy outside marriage or religious families whose daughters had committed sins of the flesh were very prone to produce birth mothers who experienced a lot of guilt:

You know, you cannot escape the feeling when you are a Christian that you have actually sinned by sleeping with somebody before you are married, which now I think is totally and utterly ridiculous, but I was twenty years old, I was brought up in a religious background in a religious country ... but you carry the guilt around with you, you definitely do.

And if you are guilty, it seems only right that you should be punished. Molly was in no doubt about this:

When I did get pregnant there was a feeling of satisfaction there. I was pregnant and I was glad to be punished for it; I was so guilty about sex, practically had to get drunk to be able to do it! I knew I was pregnant within a couple of weeks. Some people don't know for a really long time or they pretend to themselves; they really astonish me. I see them as fairly unguilty kinds of people. I'm so guilty, or I was then, that I lived in the expectation of punishment! Early sex! It's awful, so unnecessary. Being desperate to see whether I menstruated or not. So terrified. A few days late. Being in a panic.

(Inglis, 1984, p.53)

Feeling Alone

If the reaction of other people was felt to be hostile and rejecting, the unmarried mother-to-be realized that essentially she was going to be alone with her pregnancy. Parents and partners were often more concerned about how the pregnancy would reflect on *them* and less willing or able to put themselves in the shoes of the birth mother and recognize the full import of what was happening to her. A feeling of isolation began to haunt those mothers who were told that they had made their bed so they would have to lie on it. This was particularly hard and frightening for those who were young and strangers to life beyond the shelter of the family. 'The worst bit was feeling completely alone; total isolation,' recalled Samantha. 'I was on my own going through all of this nightmare and nobody seemed to know or care and I could hardly believe it was all really happening to me.' Jeanette said, 'Here I was totally friendless, pregnant in a strange city, feeling absolutely worthless.' It was her nineteenth birthday and she just felt numb. 'I kept thinking this wouldn't be happening if there wasn't something wrong with me' (Inglis, 1984, p.86).

Hazy Days and Crazy Days

Although a number of the storytellers remembered the days of their pregnancy in vivid detail – 'it's something you never ever forget' – it was just as likely that the birth mother had only a vague recollection of what had taken place at that time. Many said that they felt as if they were in a 'dream'. Rather like the disbelief and denial that surrounded the possibility of being pregnant, it was as if these mothers had blocked out the awful memories of that time; they could recall few details and had a hazy notion that perhaps their pregnancy was too painful to remember. 'It's really strange,' puzzled Iris; 'I just couldn't remember when she was born, the date, I mean, or how I got to the hospital. It was as if I was floating along in some kind of dream, and I was me and not me, if you know what I mean.' Prue agreed:

> After that it all got very hazy; like stepping on to a conveyor belt that no one else can see. I was in a dream just drifting into a

situation where I stopped making decisions, stopped being afraid, just stopped. It was like being another person.

(Inglis, 1984, p.26)

The advice that the birth mother should try to forget all about the pregnancy and the baby was clearly successful in many cases. Patti said, 'that it was as if it had happened to somebody else. I just can't associate everything that happened then with what I am now. Oh, I am a pleasant, attractive, well-groomed mother of two. Solicitor's wife. Who am I? Oh, I don't really know that. The older I get, the more I realize how much I've been shaped by everybody else' (Shawyer, 1979, p.141).

But if the details of the pregnancy remained vague in the memory for some, others recall a time of major activity. New places, new faces; changes in role, changes in shape; a world suddenly turned upside down. These were crazy days in which there was great panic, fear and excitement. Sophia's story illustrates how frenetic this time can be. Here is a shortened version of her life up to the day she delivered her daughter:

The funny thing is that I have a tendency to blank out things to do with adoption and to do with birth and everything because I went through such a terrible time emotionally . . . I'd never been allowed to go out with boys, and I went off to university and sort of completely went off the rails . . . After university, I eventually ended up in Sheffield. I was twenty-three, a pretty immature twenty-three . . . I moved around a bit and did my sort of hippy thing . . . After one disastrous relationship in Bristol I walked into a local pub and immediately met this chap. I mean it all sounds like a romance story. I went back with him that night and moved into his flat. I was completely bowled over by it. He'd been married, had children and now he was on his own, working in the classical music and jazz field. He was older than me. I'd never known a sophisticated man of the world before and it was a complete education. And within two months he said to me 'I'll marry you as soon as my divorce comes through, and I want you to have my child,' because he was missing his children. So it was the only time I'd made love without any form of protection and I got pregnant straight away . . .

. . . By the time it was obvious he was in all sorts of financial rack and ruin, bailiffs were coming to the door taking things away and I was fending them off . . . And after I announced I was pregnant he started spending the odd night out, which broke my heart, you know, because I suspected he was going with other women, and I thought, 'How could he, he loves me, I'm having his child' . . .

. . . When I was three months pregnant, this girl came to the door who looked like a blonde-haired version of me. And she said, 'Who are you?' I said, 'I'm Pete's fiancée,' and she said, 'No, you're not. I'm Pete's fiancée.' So I said, 'Well, excuse me, I'm his fiancée, and what's more I'm pregnant by him.' And she said, 'Well, I've got a two-year-old son by him and he's going to marry me.' We stood there like two cats on the doorstep, and you know my world was just crashing around my ears at the rate of knots. I said, 'Well, you'd better come in.' So we ended up getting heartily drunk saying what a bastard he was and crying all over each other and then she went home. When I told him about her he tried to gloss over it: 'Oh, I finished with her ages ago.' But then I met another girl who had had two abortions because of him and I became aware that he was a complete lecher. Oh, I felt utterly crushed. I was still prepared to stay with him because I was blind with love but then the next thing was the house was repossessed. He went back to live with his parents and I had to find somewhere else to stay . . . An old university friend put me up in Manchester.

I inquired about an abortion but the doctor said I was sixteen weeks pregnant and he wouldn't do it and so I tried to get a back-street one which was absolutely revolting and didn't work. So I spent the rest of the six months thinking I might have damaged the child, which was awful . . . The friend's flat in Manchester was grotty but it was a roof over my head. Peter never got in touch. It broke my heart. He didn't answer the telephone so I phoned the next-door neighbour who said, 'I hate to tell you this but the day he moved you out, he moved a different girl in.' Well, this is going to sound absolutely awful; I decided I was going to kill him. I felt so strongly. I got the sharpest knife out of the kitchen, I stuck it in my handbag, and I got the next train to Bristol. When I got there I went into a pub, drank two bottles of cider to try and give myself Dutch courage, walked all the way to his house, knocked on the door, and he was out! I don't know to this day what would have happened if he had been in . . . I cried all over the girl next door and then went beetling back to Manchester . . .

When I was five months I met this lovely boy. He was smashing. He didn't see I was pregnant because I was wearing something floaty and he asked me out. I met him the next night and I was wearing something different and he said, 'Oh, my God!' He saw I was wearing a wedding ring. He thought he'd dated a married pregnant woman. But he turned out to be absolutely wonderful. He didn't want to marry me or anything like that, a friendship, but he kept an eye on me all the rest of the way through, and towards the end I actually moved into his flat in Eccles Road which was literally a few doors away from the maternity home.

PARENTS

So far we have considered the birth mother's own state of mind as she contemplates her pregnancy and its profound implications. But as we have said, what she thinks and plans and feels does not take place in a social vacuum. Other people have views and offer opinions; they create the climate in which the mother-to-be either feels loved or rejected, valued or worthless, wholesome or tainted. And of all the people who may form part of the birth mother's world, none are as important and critical as her own parents. Without the institutional support of a marriage of her own, most mothers were heavily reliant on the protection, support and help of their families. Some parents rallied to their daughter's aid and made the experience of being pregnant less horrendous and less of an ordeal. Sandra, pregnant at the age of fifteen, appreciated her mother and father sticking by her:

Mum and Dad were great, actually. They were a great source of support and it was tough for them. I think they tried to leave it up to me, but obviously it's very hard to make a decision when you're that young. They didn't put any pressure on me really; they were really good. Whatever decision I made I think they would have stuck by me.

Sandra was lucky. Most daughters, far from receiving parental support, suffered their anger, upset and hurt. *The birth mother had let her parents down*; she had brought shame and disgrace to the family:

> The father of my son, whom I loved at the time, wanted to marry me and was very excited about the future arrival of our child ... When approaching my parents for permission, we were refused, saying we were too young and I had brought disgrace upon the family and I should be thrown in the gutter. My mother even took me to a psychiatrist for my so-called sexual problem, to find out if I was a normal, healthy child.
>
> (Shawyer, 1979, p.108)

Angela's mother telephoned her daughter and in a very distraught voice told her not to come home. '"Whatever you do," she said, "don't come home, I don't want the neighbours to know, promise me. We don't want this shame to get round the family." She literally sent me £50 hush money!' Throughout these accounts, time and again the parents' overriding concern was the distress their daughter's pregnancy was going to cause *them*, as parents, and the horror they felt at the thought of the shame and ignominy that were about to fall on their shoulders. 'The great thing,' said Janet, 'was that nobody was to know; the neighbours weren't to know and it was all to be kept very secret.' Parents felt that they had 'trusted' their daughter and she had 'let them down'. What had they done to deserve such treatment? Mary's father was beside himself when he was told that she was pregnant:

> I was my father's favourite and he was for drowning himself. When he found out that I was pregnant he went crazy. 'Get your coat on,' he says. And my mother said, 'Where are you taking her?' 'I'll take her to the river, her and I are going to the river.' He was so upset, and he kept repeating over and over again, 'How could you do this to me? Don't you know how much I loved you?' And my mother said, trying to make light of it, she said, 'She won't be needing her coat if she's going to jump in the river!' And we all laughed even though it was so serious ... And my father

took me out in the car and I was shaking and we stopped and he said, 'Mary, I won't speak to you no more,' he said, 'I won't. You've hurt me so much.'

Hurt soon turned to anger and, in some cases, abuse. Parents expressed disgust at their daughter's behaviour. She would be accused of being a whore and a slut. She was a moral pariah who had to be removed from social view; she had misbehaved, she was 'in trouble' and so she had to be punished. Joy, seventeen years old, told her mother that she was six months pregnant. 'She turned her back before I'd said it properly and then she turned round with this real nasty look and yelled at me, "Get out of here, you slut. I knew this would happen, get away, I can't stand the sight of you"' (Inglis, 1984, p.32). Christine became pregnant after her very first experience of sexual intercourse. Her boyfriend said he thought the condom he had been using must have fallen off. She was fifteen. Christine's doctor confirmed the pregnancy and said he would break the news to her mother:

My mum came and picked me up and she just started on at me, and I feel from that point she destroyed me. She dropped me off at home and she went on to one of her gym-club meetings that was run by the local school. I just sat and cried all night. I was in a right state. My dad held me and I just couldn't stop crying, and my dad held me again, but my mother obviously didn't like that. She told him not to hold me and he's never touched me to this day since. And after that when I got home from school I used to cry, I used to cry all night literally. They never looked at me, nothing, you know. I was just ignored the whole time . . .
 . . . My mum had had a very different life. She couldn't accept me being pregnant but she was so horrible. It was 'Oh, you're so dirty. You need to keep washing yourself. You won't be clean again. Nobody will ever want you. You'll never have a white wedding', which didn't bother me, but to her it was the end of the world. 'Nobody will ever want you, no mother will ever let their son go out with you again.'
The minute I finished my O levels I was shut in a bedroom; the neighbours weren't supposed to see me. If anybody came to the door I ran up and hid in my bedroom. I wasn't supposed to go out

in the garden in case the neighbours saw me. The vicar used to come, and I'll never forgive him for this. The vicar and my mum and dad used to sit in the back room and have prayer sessions about me. The vicar never spoke to me, not once. And I felt as if I had got evil inside me because I remember walking in there – my mum, dad and the vicar at this prayer session – and I was told to get out and I felt like I'd got real evil inside me ...

By about six months I felt the baby kick. I felt the glow of being pregnant. One day I was at my friend Judith's house who lived near the school, and her dad drove me home and he was very kind. But when I got back my mum said, 'Oh, has it gone down the toilet then?' I said 'No'. And she said, 'Oh, wouldn't it be lovely if it had,' and all I felt was this baby kicking about inside me.

Banished

For the sake of appearances, many young pregnant women were sent away from home. A heavy, inexorable logic underpinned this decision. The unmarried mother and her parents would be saved from shame and embarrassment. The 'spoiled identity' would be managed by the simple expedient of removing it to another place where the mother was not known. Unlike the married woman, who was happy to show the world that she was pregnant and the world was happy to see her so, the unmarried woman was expected to lead an altogether more furtive life, with her head hung in shame and with no one saying 'congratulations' and 'how happy we are for you'. Once the baby was born and placed for adoption, the unmarried mother could return home to resume her life as if nothing had happened. People would not speak of the baby, either because the subject was profoundly uncomfortable for them or they simply knew nothing of the child. To all intents and purposes her pregnancy was made 'invisible'. The aim was to pretend that it had never really happened. The contrast between the married mother's pregnancy and the unmarried mother's pregnancy could hardly be more stark. Dismay contrasts with joy, the future is faced with foreboding and not with excitement. Having a baby, especially a first baby, is a highly significant event and the way it is greeted and experienced has lasting implications.

For a pregnancy to be treated as a dirty thing which has to be hidden away from view and then later denied leaves wounds which do not always heal.

'I just knew I would be banished,' recollected a mother, 'and I was. I was six weeks pregnant and I was sent away. Now I wonder why I was sent away so early. Nobody could tell I was pregnant. But my family knew, so I had to go. It was almost like I was contagious' (Rockel and Ryburn, 1988, pp.24–5). Relatives who lived far away were a good place to send errant daughters. However, the pregnant woman had to know her place, be grateful, suitably subdued, contrite and always humble. She was in no position to hold her head up high. She was very dependent on the generosity of others and if they felt that she must be helped to see the error of her ways, then she must accept this quietly and with grace. She was, after all, a fallen woman.

Molly said that her parents had 'arranged for me to live with my sister and her husband. He's an ex-priest and my sister was going to be a nun and they are both very Catholic. It was horrible because their idea was that they were doing this wonderful deed for this dreadful person. I was quite pleased to leave and go into this unmarried mothers' home' (Inglis, 1984, p.55). Joy was sent to 'a home for girls in trouble'. 'It was all right, I suppose; I mean they didn't yell at me or anything but all the time you know you were real low, in trouble, and that you couldn't complain about anything or tell anyone what you felt like. Most of the girls were real humble, creeping around with those looks on their faces' (ibid., p.33). But Janet did feel her 'home for unmarried mothers' was punitive and she did not enjoy her time there:

I actually think that really I had no choice. I don't remember ever considering staying at home, and it was to everybody's great relief that there was a place I could actually go to for all the pregnancy and not just six weeks at the end. The assumption was that you were there to be away from home and you could go back home in the state in which people saw you leave. I just know I wouldn't have been allowed in the house with my parents with me getting more pregnant as the months went by. Their only way of surviving was for me not to be there ... The place was very, very punitive, absolutely awful. We didn't question how punitive it was at the time. We knew mother and baby homes were to punish you for being bad, so I knew it would be like that.

OTHER PEOPLE

Further confirmation of the birth mother's changed and reduced status came from the reaction of friends and people who knew that the pregnancy was taking place outside marriage. If the reaction was negative, and it often was, the mother-to-be received a further dose of hurt and a further reminder that she had to start rethinking what kind of person she had become. 'During that period,' said Patti, 'my best friend got married, but she didn't invite me to the wedding. That hurt me... *She* was still a nice girl' (Shawyer, 1979, p.130). However, one of Prue's male friends was not put off by her pregnancy, and although his offer of help could not be accepted, it was well meant: 'My real friend said very generously that he'd marry me but I thought that was hopeless. Ridiculous again, I loved him but the baby wasn't his and I felt guilty about that. It felt like imposing' (Inglis, 1984, p.25).

Although many of the women who went to homes for unmarried mothers said that their experience was an unhappy one and that those in charge were punitive, this wasn't always the case. Patti described the home that she went to as beautiful. The matron was 'very nice' and although many of the women played up their role as 'bad girls', nevertheless the staff were not uncaring or hostile. As we have heard, Janet did find her 'home' punitive, but she met people who were friendly. While they were only a few months pregnant, the women had to go out to work:

You had to be doing paid work. They had an arrangement with an agency in Birmingham and we all went along and were given titles of Mrs. We all got provided with a Woolworth wedding ring and found jobs in factories and our money paid our rent for living in the home. The home was run by two women. One was quite reasonably warm but the other was an absolute pig. We had to be in by six, in bed by ten, no visitors. You were allowed to see people on Saturday afternoon between two and five. The rest of the time you had to live on the premises and on Sundays you had to go to church . . . I worked in a small mail-order factory with some really working-class girls who hadn't got the sort of background I'd got. And they were so kind to me. I mean, when I told them I was pregnant and the situation I was in, their mothers used to send me food parcels! They knitted things for me and they were so kind and close to me.

But generally it was rare for the birth mother to meet many other people. The strategy was to remove her from social circulation. The only other people she was likely to encounter were those in the health and welfare field. Those who attended antenatal classes often reported a cool reception: 'Unmarried mothers didn't go to pre-natal classes,' was Chris's memory, 'especially with babies for adoption. Bad enough to be unmarried, but for adoption, well! Single mothers don't get the same pre-natal care and people think it's because they are slack about it but it's this sort of thing that puts them off.' She felt they were uncomfortable when she attended. 'They just assume we don't care about our babies, that we're not looking after them before they are born. There is just this stupid assumption that a baby for adoption is a baby not cared about' (Inglis, 1984, p.116). Shawyer echoes this feeling from her own experience as an unmarried mother. She felt health workers assumed that her baby would be of no worth or importance to her. As she writes, her indignation and outrage increase as she compares the lot of the married and the unmarried mother: 'The married mother who enjoys security in her emotional, financial and social situation receives *extra* support. The single woman with *no* emotional support and in an extremely tenuous social and financial situation is not only given no support at all, but she also receives a resounding vote of "no confidence" from her family and the rest of society. No confidence in her as a person; no confidence in her ability to parent her own child. At the time she needs it most, she loses all belief in herself and, when that moment comes she will passively "consent" to adoption' (Shawyer, 1979, p.16).

THE FATHER OF THE UNBORN CHILD

In many ways the father of the baby is not portrayed as a particularly significant character in the birth mother's story. It is not so much that he wasn't loved or liked at the time, for often he was, but once the woman found herself pregnant and unable or unwilling to marry him, he became of no practical use in helping her cope with the consequences. In some instances he was only a young man himself, possibly still at school with the mother. In other cases he was a married man or a feckless, insubstantial individual that the woman did not wish to marry. Of course, if she did marry him, the mother would join the ranks of the righteous and acceptable, and there would be no adoption. It was because this route was not chosen or not available that her situation took on a different and altogether more sombre hue. With the increasing urgency of sorting out what to do and where to go, the birth father became of less interest and relevance. As the birth mother necessarily became preoccupied with her own worries, he would find that there was little room in the saga for him and often he completely disappeared from the story. This upset and angered some mothers but not a few viewed his departure neutrally and with no great interest.

This confused, rather hesitant view of the father as someone whose role ranged from being supportive and concerned to hostile or irrelevant is confirmed by Raynor's findings (1971, p.17). A third of the mothers in the study chose to deal with the pregnancy without involving the putative father. Indeed, most of these mothers never even told the man.

> Of the fathers who had been consulted about plans, four or five had been very supportive to the mother. Five others had made the suggestion that the baby should be adopted, thirty-one agreed with the mother that it was the best plan, and three felt that the decision should rest entirely with the mother. Five fathers offered marriage with a view to keeping the baby, but the mothers did not agree. Fourteen fathers were thought to be uninterested, and thirteen were said to oppose the adoption . . .

In our interviews Sheila said that Doug had been 'quite supportive in his own way, I mean, he never pushed me one way or the other to keep her or get rid of her or whatever. He was quite happy for his mum to bring her up, but on the other hand he never kept a stable job, he was violent and just immature really.'

Less honourable was Jim. He was nineteen and three years older than Margaret. He had pestered her for sex and after a while she acquiesced and almost immediately found herself pregnant:

> He came round to see me once a week and he told me we'd get married, what his mum and dad had said when he told them, and what his sister had said. He took me out for a drive in his car and he showed me a house that belonged to a friend of his whose dad was a farmer and had lots of land and this lad had said we could have this house to rent. We'll go abroad, he said. We'll do this, we'll do that. You can go and do your A levels at college in the evenings. Full of stories like that . . . When I was seven and a half months pregnant Jim just stopped coming round to see me. Just stopped coming. I phoned him up several times and he just pretended he was his dad saying he wasn't in and things like that. I cried a lot over that.

Several of the mothers in the book by Inglis were angry with and confused by the cowardly behaviour of the fathers of their babies. When Prue told her 'guy' he became very hostile. He knew she didn't love him and so he questioned the baby's paternity.

> Men are so bloody slippery . . . I assumed he'd believe me. I was pretty hopeless. Weepy and guilty; somehow it was my fault, his attitude made it more my fault. I wasn't particularly hung up about sex but I did feel I should at least love him. Well, I didn't, and instead of that helping it made it worse.

(Inglis, 1984, p.25)

Derek was twenty and Joy was seventeen when she got pregnant. Initially she was in love with him but she quickly learned that he was thoroughly 'selfish' as well as essentially weak. All he could think about when she told him she was pregnant was that they could now have sex 'without any worries'. Joy was more scared than angry:

> I turned against him. I mean I didn't think of him as any use any more . . . I could see what he was up to, trying to get away with it.

No blame. Nothing to do with him ... He just got away with it ... I don't hate him, though. I just think he's a piss-weak turd. I don't think about him, really. He's nothing special as far as men go.

(ibid., p.36)

One fifteen-year-old father did not want to talk about the pregnancy. 'Well I suppose he wouldn't have known what to do,' reflected the mother, 'he was probably as scared as me' (Rockel and Ryburn, 1988, p.36). But another birth mother was less forgiving. Even though he came to see her a couple of times, she said she was bitter: 'He had no right to father a child when he was a married man already' (ibid.).

Once the baby had been born and placed for adoption, the birth father was rarely mentioned again. He becomes a shadowy figure. The pain was left with the mother; the bad luck was all hers. Whereas his life would remain unscathed, the mother's would never be the same again.

THE UNBORN CHILD

One more person played a part in the way the mother experienced her pregnancy: the unborn baby. In spite of the horror and fear that most mothers felt when they realized that they were pregnant, most began to form a relationship with their unborn child. Often he or she was the only person who consistently made them feel good and worthwhile. The baby was helpless, unwanted and seemingly unloved by almost everyone and only she, as the mother, stood between him or her and the hostile world outside. She felt protective towards her baby. Whereas everyone else seemed intent on judging, devaluing and punishing the mother, the unborn child needed her and gave her value and worth. The baby was one of the few positive experiences in an otherwise unfriendly nine months. Nineteen of the twenty mothers interviewed by Rynearson (1982) confessed that they talked to their baby. They conducted 'an intensive private monologue with the foetus', often fantasizing that they and the child would somehow be 'saved' from the horrors of relinquishment and adoption.

Molly began to feel 'defensive for the baby. The injustice of not being welcome ... coming into the world and there was just this dreadful silence about it. The only words spoken about it were "Isn't it sad", "What a shame" ... I feel incredibly sad about it, very sensitive and finally angry ...' (Inglis, 1984, p:55). Amongst the many hundreds of letters received by Sorosky *et al.* (1978, pp.55–6) was one from a woman who got pregnant when she was sixteen. She described herself as young, inexperienced and scared:

> My seventeen-year-old boyfriend had fantasies about marriage but was really more interested in his car. My parents eventually found out and sent me to a maternity home. I did a lot of lonely meditating during those eight months. My only companion was my baby inside. We cried together. I grew older by a hundred years. My parents said that keeping the baby would ruin my life. The social worker agreed. No one really thought about what it meant to me to give her up.

In such ways the baby became the mother's only true and reliable friend, someone who was always there and able to listen. 'I had no one else,' said Pat (Arms, 1990, p.159), 'and she would listen.'

4

The Most Difficult Decision

By the time the baby is born, the birth mother is familiar with how others now regard her; she has learned who she is and what this means. In the final months of her pregnancy the mother is left with few doubts about how other people view both her and the baby. These same people continue to feature in the birth mother's life at the time of the birth and immediately afterwards. These are days when the full reality of being an unmarried mother hit home and this is the time when she has to decide whether to keep the baby or not. If other people have defined who she is, they also begin to influence what she should do. She begins to feel that she is losing control over her life as other people appear to be determining both her identity and her actions. She experiences an increasing sense of powerlessness and finds herself being channelled towards adoption by a determined gang of social, emotional and practical pressures. In the end, adoption seems inevitable.

One of her compelling needs is to talk about what is happening, even shout about what she is thinking and feeling, but few people see this as either appropriate or necessary. Her prime condition is that of an unmarried mother with a baby. This is the grim business about which a decent silence should be maintained. The atmosphere is funereal rather than celebratory, and the soon-to-be-bereaved are expected to behave in a suitably subdued manner, particularly the person who has brought about the unhappy situation.

The complex emotional climate that arises out of these feelings and attitudes affects the quality of the birth experience, confuses the mother's maternal responses, interferes with her ability to think clearly about what to decide, and hinders the chances of her making a reasonable recovery both in the short and the long term. Once again, the birth mother's own parents often play a key role in determining how she copes with having the baby and decides on his or her future. But other players also enter the stage, and can make the experience of early motherhood more or less difficult. Doctors and midwives can affect the mother. Her baby, now alive and kicking, vulnerable and appealing, clearly complicates the emotional equation. Social workers proffer views on what might be best for babies born outside marriage to young, unsupported mothers. And at the centre of the dilemma and the target for other people's advice and feelings is the birth mother. She has undergone the physical effort of having a baby, her achievements in the delivery room are viewed with dismay rather than delight, she is not the focus of loving attention, she is not the subject of hearty congratulations, and on top of all this she is required to contemplate and instigate the loss of her newborn baby. This is an extraordinarily tough time for the mother. Her feelings are pulled in all directions. Whichever way she jumps, problems seem to loom. And yet, we have to keep reminding ourselves, to a large degree her experiences are the product of other people's attitudes and responses: to be unmarried and having a baby is bad; you will not be supported. To abandon your baby for adoption is bad; you are a suspect woman. The loss of your baby is a problem of your own making; do not expect any sympathy and certainly do not expect anyone to talk about it. It all seems terribly unfair, and so it is.

In the words of Suzanne Arms (1983), these mothers show us what it is like 'to love and let go'. We now follow the birth mother's story through three more stages: the birth, the decision to have the baby adopted and the immediate feelings of loss after relinquishment.

THE BIRTH

As well as the reaction of other people to the birth, the mother has to contend with her own feelings, and these are often confused. However, they are confused partly because of her own doubts about whether to relinquish her baby and partly because other people are reacting to the event in such a grim-faced fashion. All the instincts and social conventions surrounding birth normally encourage people to be cheerful, but these feelings are suppressed in the case of the mother contemplating adoption. The mother's achievement is a dubious one. She receives further confirmation that what she has done and what she has become is both unfortunate and regrettable. It is little wonder that the mother does not know whether to hold and cuddle her baby or have the child removed from her sight, whether to let her maternal feelings flow in full spate or hold them back knowing that she will soon lose the child, or whether to hate the baby for causing her so much pain or lovingly protect the infant from a hostile world.

The anecdotal evidence suggests that most mothers do not remember the birth as a particularly happy occasion. In some peculiar way, those who suffered a harsh and lonely birth felt that it was deserved; it was a proper punishment for what they had done and were about to do. But again, there are heartfelt exceptions that show that things can be different, and so, before we record the unhappier experiences, it is appropriate to mention a couple of examples where the birth is remembered as a happy event. Helen had her daughter during the middle of a cyclone in a small maternity hospital.

> There was a very nice doctor and they treated me exceedingly well; they put me in a private room which was all very pleasant. The staff were all very good, they knew all about me but they weren't maudlin or judgemental, they were just very, very nice.
>
> (Inglis, 1984, p.46)

However, even in this hospital, there was a policy at the time that mothers who were going to have their babies adopted should not see them. The babies were removed and it was not expected that the mothers would care for them. When Helen asked to see her daughter she was told that it was not allowed and that people did not think it was a 'good thing', but a soft-hearted sister relented saying, 'Oh, well, yes. You're all right, you've got it all together,' and so Helen went off to visit the nursery and see her baby. Joan's mother was present at the birth of her grandson and 'she was really good; it was very good to have someone there who was pleased for me even though he was going to be adopted'. It was a straightforward birth. The midwife was a 'nice woman who I think must have known how odd I was feeling. She didn't say much, you know, but she smiled in a sort of way that told me that she knew I was both sad and happy, you know, tears of joy and tears of sadness all at the same time. I looked after Simon before he went off to be adopted and looking back I'm really glad I did.'

More typical were the mothers who felt that a punitive atmosphere surrounded the birth of their baby. Medical staff treated the mother in a rough, condemnatory fashion that was both physically and emotionally very hurtful. The nursing sister was 'brutal', recollected Molly. She said things like 'you girls get what you deserve' (ibid., p.57). 'The doctor arrived,' wrote a mother to Shawyer (1979, p.109). 'He had no time for us bad girls. He was rough and unfeeling, and he decided to use me as a guinea-pig. He injected me all around my opening to deaden the pain of the child's head coming through. Until that moment I was quite comfortable and relaxed, but those injections! I'll never forget that pain.'

Not a few mothers felt that all their labours had been in vain. The end result of a vast amount of physical effort and pain was, to all intents and purposes, nothing, 'not even a "well done" or "congratulations"'. The mother felt alone during the baby's birth; she felt that she was on her own to face one of the most important experiences of her life. 'It was quiet, hushed, nobody dared talk,' said a mother, '. . . I suppose it *was* like a stillbirth really, because it wasn't my baby – I wasn't going to have it – and everybody was embarrassed and didn't know what to say' (Rockel and Ryburn, 1988, p.27). All that effort 'and no baby to hold at the end of it. Just an empty feeling.' This feeling of suffering for no purpose was compounded for those mothers who were not allowed to see their baby after delivery. 'Labour lasted six hours. I felt that someone was ripping my insides. My body, heart and soul were no longer whole. As soon as she was out, they whisked her away. I was so shattered. I figured I had no right to see her' (Sorosky et al., 1978, p.56). Sheila was only sixteen when she had her daughter. 'The experience of that was pretty horrible. They insisted on calling me Mrs and I said they had to call me Miss. After the baby was born they just took her away and when I came to, I said where's my baby and they said "Oh, we've taken her away because she's going to be adopted" and I couldn't believe they could just do that and that I was not important in all of this.' Pamela, too, was discouraged from seeing her daughter:

Carla was born at ten past four in the morning. I was on my own
with a nurse who was very nice to me. Carla was taken away
immediately. I was taken back to the ward. The other babies were
brought in about ten past seven and I asked where my baby was.
And everybody ignored me, as if I wasn't there. When I said to
the nurses, 'I want to see my baby,' I eventually had to get out of
bed and go searching through cupboards and rooms until I found
her. She was put in a room all on her own. And the nurse came
running and she said, 'You're not to touch that baby. That baby's
for adoption.' I quickly grabbed hold of her and brought her back
to my bed and I wouldn't let her out of my sight ... I was
frightened to death they might steal her from me.

(ITV, 1990)

Some were not sure about whether they wanted to see their
baby or not. Raynor (1971, p.51) noted that many mothers sought
to 'depersonalize' their experience of pregnancy and birth as a
way of coping with the trauma of giving up the baby for adoption.
Once born, these mothers would try not to get involved with the
baby. Others coped by resorting to the fantasy they were actually
caring for the baby for someone else who was the 'real' mother. It
was as if the mothers felt they had forfeited any rights to their
baby; they were not entitled to feel love and affection for the
child. Patti (Shawyer, 1979, p.136) remembered that they had
given her the baby to hold. 'And I was so *embarrassed*. I just
wished they'd take her away, because I didn't know what to say. I
didn't know what to say to my baby. I knew what I would have
liked to have said. But she wasn't my baby to say it to.' At first
Mary 'did not want anything to do' with her child – 'I hated it' –
but gradually she found herself being drawn to the baby, wanting
to pick her up and nurse her.

THE DECISION

Circumstances and the people involved led the mothers to conclude that their baby should be placed for adoption. Although not
always under explicit pressure from other people, the mother
found herself unable to contemplate looking after the child without material and personal support. If these should continue to be

lacking, she felt she had little choice but to relinquish her baby. In retrospect, mothers gave four basic reasons why they chose to have their baby adopted:

1. Pressure from family and parents – 'It's for the best.'
2. Best for the baby – 'It's only fair to the child.'
3. Best for the mother – 'I had the rest of my life to think about.'
4. No practical alternative – 'What else could I do?'

1. Parental Pressure

Parents, particularly mothers, were inclined either to take charge of the adoption arrangements or to threaten their daughter with rejection if she did not have the baby adopted. Mary's mother, without her knowledge or consent, arranged for the baby to be adopted by relatives in America. 'She wrote to them saying when they were to come over and that I'm giving it up for adoption and they could come over and take the child. I knew nothing about this! Nothing! It all went on behind my back!' More subtle was the reaction of Prue's parents. Prue felt under siege. When the baby was born the almoner kept demanding that she think about whether she really was a fit person to care for the baby. In desperation she telephoned home and said '"I don't know what to do" . . . My mother said, "Come home as soon as you can" and my father said they would be so happy to see me soon and although nothing at all was said it was clear they didn't mean with a baby. Our neighbours wouldn't have liked that sort of thing going on' (Inglis, 1984, p.28). Chris had to carry her baby in and out of the house in a wash basket covered by a blanket! 'One Saturday,' she continues, 'my aunty turned up out of the blue! Panic! There was all this baby stuff, bottles and sterilizing gear. My mother rushed through the whole kitchen and wiped every bit of evidence of my baby out. Cleared the benches and bundled us into the bedroom . . .' (ibid., p.122). Alice started her story with a vigorous statement about why her baby was adopted:

> Before I say anything else, what I'd really like to point out is that many of us give up our child to please our families, because the

families were putting pressure on us. So mothers give up their child; they lose their child but the relationship they have with their family before the child was born never comes back, so, in other words, it was a waste of time. You lost the child and your family, so you might as well have kept your child.

Rita felt that she was carried along by the expectations and assumptions of those around her. In their highly exposed and vulnerable condition, many birth mothers recall with shock their own passivity and apparent powerlessness at the time. The most important decision of their lives was taken out of their hands, or so it felt:

My dad said that if I came home with her, my baby, he'd leave . . . At the time I felt detached. There had been a script written and I didn't consider that there could be another one. I mean the only thing I felt at all was angry with those who were keeping their babies, and I felt angry with them because they had broken the rules and they weren't keeping to my script . . . At the time I was being told that I was not fit to have a baby and to be a single parent. All the messages I'd been given were not to be like this which was why she was to be adopted, to give her a nice happy home, and to live with nice parents. I think I was trying to deny the fact that I did have a choice.

2. Best for the Baby

A range of people were likely to advise the mother that adoption was the best course of action – 'It's only fair to the baby.' The clear implication contained in this advice was that the birth mother was not the best person to bring up the child. For a mother, this is a devastating judgement and is calculated to undermine not only her confidence but her self-esteem too. Social workers spent a lot of time helping the mother decide whether or not she should place the baby for adoption. But once the decision had been made to surrender the child, many mothers felt that the adoption worker lost all interest in them and concentrated entirely on the baby. The birth mothers had produced the baby and once the decision had been made, they were out of the picture and of no further interest. 'I felt that the social worker gave me all the information about childless couples,' reflected Sandra, 'and how short they were of babies, in short supply, you know, as if she was sort of keen to get hold of my baby. But I suppose it was the way it felt at the time . . . I think in the end I knew in my heart that I would give her up . . . I had to do what was best for the child. You had to think of her future.'

Lurking beneath the surface of many of the discussions between the mother and the 'professionals' was a pernicious double-bind: if you really love your baby you will give him or her up for adoption; if you keep the child then that is proof that you do not sincerely have his or her best interests at heart and therefore you are not a fit person to care for the baby. One of the mothers who wrote to Sorosky *et al.* (1978, p.61) said, 'I was told I had nothing to offer the child that was to be born and that if I loved her I would give her up so that she could have a home and parents. I am very bitter and resentful of the pressure put on me.' Many mothers reported that they thought because they had been bad, immoral and had failed their child, they had no real right to say that they wanted to keep the baby or even take charge of the decision about whether to have the child adopted or not. This argument was certainly used against some mothers, as the following letter shows:

The matron kept on saying, 'Stop thinking about yourself. Think of the baby. It should be brought up in a home with a mother and a father, and think of the joy he would give to this couple who want to adopt your baby. They can't have children, you can have plenty in the future.' Mum's argument was, 'You got yourself into trouble, you have to pay the consequences. I'm not having you home with the baby. What will the neighbours say? I'm not working to support you. I've had enough of children, they are nothing but trouble. No man will want to marry you once he finds out that you have had a baby.' I got nowhere and felt like everyone was against me, and so they were.

(Shawyer, 1979, p.110)

However, it was not unusual for some mothers to view the decision to have the baby adopted in a positive light. This did not mean that the decision was any easier, but after taking a deep breath it seemed that adoption would be the best way forward for all concerned. These mothers made what for them was a realistic appraisal of what they could and could not do for the baby. They accepted the argument that to give their baby to a competent couple was in itself an act of love. 'I put the new outfit on him, took some pictures and held him for the last time. It was hard, but I knew I had done the best possible thing for both of us. That was three and a half months ago' (Sorosky *et al.*, 1978, p.62). Another mother seemed to have all the odds stacked against her; she had a baby when she was sixteen, her parents disowned her, she worked and looked after her baby at weekends. But in the end it all proved too much: 'I felt I wasn't being fair to her; I felt I was being selfish wanting to hang on to her' (Shawyer, 1979, p.102). In spite of the sadness, there was a sense of relief:

> I can honestly say I don't regret it. That doesn't mean it was easy or I didn't love her. I do love her, but I couldn't have looked after her then the way I would have wanted to. I wouldn't have known how. I mean eight years ago I was just a schoolgirl. When I decided on adoption it was a huge relief really. I knew it was the only way to give her the things I wanted her to have.
>
> (Rockel and Ryburn, 1988, p.140)

These stories begin to merge with those in which the mother was thinking about her own future as much as that of her baby. But before we hear what these mothers have to say, there is one special category that needs to be mentioned. Women who became mothers through rape and incest often had very mixed and confused feelings about their baby. In some cases, the baby wins through and is loved for himself or herself. In other cases, the baby is a powerful reminder of the terrible circumstances that gave rise to his or her existence. In Chris's case, although she did not get pregnant by her father, she and her sister had been sexually abused by him over many years. She simply could not contemplate bringing up her own daughter while she was still living at home: 'You see the only way for me to survive was to rely on the family to some extent and I certainly wasn't going to bring up a girl, or a boy for that matter, in that house or in that family. It was just not on' (Inglis, 1984, pp.115–16).

3. Best for the Mother

It was very clear to a few women that keeping their baby would change their lives to an extent that was not acceptable. The sacrifice they would have to make would not only be too great, but it would adversely affect their feelings towards the child who had brought about their reduced condition. Louise was nineteen when she had her daughter. She wanted to keep the baby but she could not stand the thought of being a poor, struggling mother. The decision to surrender the baby was difficult and it 'hurt like hell'. But if she kept the baby, Louise was in no doubt that her life would have come to a 'full stop' (Inglis, 1984, p.145). Dora's life had been getting progressively messier and the birth of her son was the last straw. She knew that if she did not have him adopted not only might she sink without trace but the baby would go down with her 'and what would be the point of that?' Looking back she saw the birth of Jeremy as a turning-point in her life. The irony was not lost on Dora that the fondness and gratitude that she still feels towards her son were founded on her decision to relinquish him for adoption and never see him again.

4. 'What Else Could I Do?'

Without parental support, without an income or a home of her own, without anyone to whom she could turn, without sensible support from the state, the birth mother felt that she had no choice but to place her baby for adoption. Her decision was not one of the heart but one of the purse. However she looked at her situation, there was no way she and her baby could survive. In refusing to support her, the world left her no alternative. As we shall hear in the next chapter, many mothers never forgive 'the world' for forcing them to give up their child and of all the people in the world who might have helped, the birth mother is least likely to forgive her own parents for failing her at this critical point in her life.

'I'm a teacher, I'm unmarried, I have no prospects of being married, I couldn't support it, there's no way I could return to my family; they didn't and wouldn't want anything to do with it.' Helen could only conclude that 'it would be just *appalling* for everybody! So I said adoption was the only thing' (Inglis, 1984, p.44). This sense of mounting hopelessness and desperation is heard over and over again. The mother, seeringly tempted to keep her baby, sees only an abyss before her and the only way to prevent herself and the baby plunging into chaos is to give up the child. This way both live, but a heavy emotional price has to be paid. It was not unusual for mothers to be surprised at how much they loved the baby once he or she had been born. This, of course, made the decision even more difficult. Three quarters of the mothers who placed their baby for adoption in Raynor's study said that caring for the child had made giving up the baby much harder. In similar vein, nearly all of the mothers who decided to keep their babies said caring for the child had been a factor in their decision (Raynor, 1971, pp.32–3). The mothers had not bargained for the power of their feelings towards the child. Sophia desperately tried to treat her daughter as an 'object' to make the parting less painful, but she failed: 'I just wanted to pick her up and cuddle her, I knew which was her cry in the nursery. It just broke my heart.' Many of the accounts record how the mothers would steal out of their hospital beds in the middle of the night just to see and touch their baby. The situation remained impossible but their love for the baby demanded that the child be kept.

> After Mark was born Mum came, and they brought him in and plonked him down. He was a really big baby. Enormous. I couldn't believe it and I said, 'Can I keep him?' Mum burst into tears. I had too much pride to say – I really wanted to scream it out – 'Look, I want him. He's my baby.' Wanting something that's your very own, that's a strong thing. When Mark was born he was mine, he was somebody that didn't have any prejudice against me.
>
> (Shawyer, 1979, pp.151–2)

Age, people and money all had to be right if the mother was going to have any prospect of keeping the baby. A serious deficiency in any one of these meant that looking after the baby was going to be a hazardous business. At sixteen Pauline knew she was too young to cope. She did not want her daughter to be adopted but she had no way of caring for her. She lived with her grandmother. Money was short and it seemed to Pauline that bit by bit she was being 'forced into a situation where I had to give her up'.

Christine had managed to care for her baby a little longer than Pauline, but she too felt the pressures mount. Her plan was to keep the baby: 'there was no way I was giving him up'. After obtaining her O levels, Christine found a job in local government. Her parents would not support the baby and so he was placed with foster parents. Christine visited him as often as she could, all the time trying to work out how she could bring him up on her own. The foster mother proved to be unhelpful: 'She was really awkward. She would say to me "Make his bottle up" but she wouldn't show me how to do it. "Change his nappy" and she would sort of plonk him on my lap and I would struggle to change him.' The foster mother was an expert in child care and Christine felt she was made to feel inadequate and incompetent before this professional. 'And then she kept saying "Oh, you've got to do what's best for the baby." Sort of blackmail.' After a period of illness over Christmas, Christine struggled to visit her son. She arrived in the town on a stormy night:

I remember waiting at the bus-stop, I just felt so pressurized and worn down by it all. I just felt it was all too much, and I got to Huddersfield station and a lot of the power lines were down and the trains were running very late, and I just sat on Huddersfield station and wept. I just thought, 'I can't fight any more, I just can't.' I phoned up my mum and dad. They were at a party with their friends there, and my dad said, 'Well, where are you?' and I said, 'Huddersfield station.' 'What are you doing there?' and I said, 'All right, I'll have him adopted then.' I just gave up, and thought, 'I can't fox any more.' My mum and dad picked me up. They were quite nice to me but that was the last time it was mentioned by them. It's never been mentioned since.

Worn down and worn out by the mounting pressure, many mothers simply gave in. They had no more energy to fight. It was easier to switch off and let other people take over. These birth mothers felt powerless to control events. 'I didn't have any fight left in me. I mean, I'd done something wrong by having a baby; now they were making me feel as though I was doing something worse by wanting to keep my own baby' (Inglis, 1984, p.93). 'I was losing all control over my life,' concluded Jackie, '. . . I let go and the whole system took over' (ibid., p.106). Birth mothers felt both 'not in control' (other people were taking over the decision-making process) and 'out of control' (life seemed to be careering along in a turbulent and frightening whirl). 'It was like being swept down a river with a continual feeling of drowning. Not having somebody look out for me. Not having control over what was happening to me' (Rockel and Ryburn, 1988, pp.27–8). Tired, defeated and demoralized, the mother became passive and acquiescent. It seemed that there was no one willing to help her keep the baby. Everyone was determined that the child must be adopted.

This was the time when the birth mother wanted to talk to people, to mull things over, to rehearse the options, but there was no one willing to listen. It seemed, to the mother at least, that there was a *conspiracy of silence*. Athough she wanted to give voice to her feelings, other people did not want to hear. She was being asked to make the hardest decision of her life and there was no one to help her talk things through. 'My parents came to visit me,' said Moira, 'but they wouldn't talk about the baby or anything. It was unreal. We'd talk about my sister and the dog, but all I wanted to do was say "I've got a baby! You're grandparents! What am I going to do?" But nothing. It was crazy. We pretended nothing really important had really happened, and I went along with it.' The silence and refusal to talk about or even acknowledge what had transpired continued once the mother returned home without her baby. Bridget's parents did visit her in hospital but 'no one congratulated me on having the baby; they were really miserable. They sat there grim-faced . . . When I went home, my mum was away for the weekend, and my dad was there. He didn't speak to me.' Family life resumed, albeit in sombre and determined mood, as if nothing of moment had happened.

THE IMMEDIATE FEELINGS OF LOSS

The first few days and weeks without the baby were remembered as both difficult and strange. The 'conspiracy of silence' continued. The major loss that the mother had experienced was acknowledged only by a determined silence. Sandra, who on the whole felt her family were very supportive, realized that the baby was not a subject that anyone was going to raise. If the adoption was ever to be mentioned at all, she would have to do it herself:

> It was a horrible feeling really. I mean, people who give up babies I think should have some kind of follow-up, but there's just nothing. You're just left and you have just given up your child and it's not a thing you talk about. Close friends and family know, and in the end you talk about it from time to time, but nobody brings the subject up. It's just a part of you that nobody talks about.

Clearly, it is not only parents who maintain the silence. Friends and colleagues seem unable to acknowledge that the mother has had a baby and that the child has been adopted. If the topic arises at all, the only response seems to be one of embarrassment. Six weeks after the baby's birth, Janet went back to work to resume her training:

> I'd had the photographs of me and the baby developed and people who knew why I had gone away didn't want to look at the photographs because they were embarrassed. They didn't know how to deal with me at all. I think I completely confounded everybody. Not so much my mum and dad because they told me what the rules were, that I didn't mention the baby and I got on with life ... My best friend was awfully embarrassed when I showed her these photographs and didn't really want to look at them.

Left with no one with whom to talk, the mother's feelings had no outlet. Her sense of loss was acute. In recollecting those early days without the baby, two feelings dominated the birth mother's emotional life: *pain* and *anger*.

Pain

A large number of mothers remained inconsolable after the baby's adoption. For each one, the unremitting pain following the loss seemed as if it would never end. It dominated her life. She could not concentrate on or settle to anything. 'I was in a terrible state, I couldn't work properly, it's a wonder they kept me on. I couldn't concentrate at all. I was severely depressed ... I just knew I felt ill and in pain' (Inglis, 1984, p.96). 'The pain of it!' exclaimed Molly. 'I didn't know what the pain of it was going to be like ... My whole body was out of whack after she was adopted ... I couldn't sleep at night at *all* ... for weeks and weeks and I would cry and cry and cry ... Nothing could ever hurt that much again – ever' (ibid., pp.58–9).

'I just couldn't stop crying' was the commonest memory. Tears would flow at the slightest upset. Comfort was hard to find, and again people were inclined to be embarrassed, even irritated, rather than concerned. 'It would have been different if people had let me be unhappy about having adopted out my baby. If they had led me to believe it was only natural for me to be unhappy. If I had had people around at the time who had just allowed me to be unhappy and to cry and to get upset, it would have been a great help to me' (Rockel and Ryburn, 1988, pp.132–3). Beryl took several months before she felt steady:

I handed over the child, I've blacked out exactly where it was, but I remember coming out and sobbing my heart out at the bus-stop and going back home ... Eventually I ended up camping out in somebody's flat and I had to give my cat away which I adored. In a way the loss of that cat represented the loss of that baby and I cried so much after the cat had gone. I realized I was getting the loss out of my system. I'd used the cat as a substitute. I'd got this little, warm, cuddly kitten to nurture.

Not a few mothers found themselves looking into prams or following women with babies, either to be near young children or to wonder if the child might be their baby. 'I found myself looking at babies in the street,' said Linda, 'wondering if they were my daughter all the time.' Babies, in fact, suddenly seemed to be everywhere:

I couldn't watch TV because the commercials would show bouncing happy babies you didn't know when. I couldn't open a magazine without babies peering at me ... I started following babies, I was feeling older and uglier every day and I'd start following a baby around the city shopping and think, that's my baby ... Then I'd see another and follow that one. All the time I was very close to a breakdown ...

(Inglis, 1984, p.99)

Anger

The hopelessness and helplessness of the situation drove some mothers to anger, anger directed against themselves for being so weak, anger against relatives who did not prevent the loss and anger against those who appeared to benefit from the adoption. Annabel remembered screaming, 'It's not bloody well fair! I've been a stupid bitch. I want my baby and I can't even bloody well get it right to look after her.' One of the mothers in Rockel and Ryburn's work said, 'I remember this hatred thing for her adoptive mother. I don't know whether that's common. She was really nice, but I used to think "That barren bitch has got my baby!" I suppose it's one way of working your anger out' (1988, pp.30–31).

Julie couldn't believe that after her baby had been born, she was expected to place the child, forget about what had happened and just carry on with her life. For a while she felt guilty about all the trouble and upset she had caused her parents. She was confused and could not stop crying:

But after a while instead of crying I seemed to be screaming all the time. I was so mad, angry, you know, that this had happened to me, that other people had decided that my baby was going to be adopted. I remember yelling at my mother saying, 'It's all your fault!' And she said that it was typical of me to blame it on her when it was me that had got into trouble and brought shame on to them all. And I thought 'She still doesn't understand, she still doesn't see what's happened.'

Although anger was quick to surface in these examples, more typically the birth mother remained subdued and tearful throughout the early days of her loss. If anger surfaced at all, it was usually many years later.

5
Living with Loss

So far we have seen what a rough road it is that the birth mother has had to travel: the stress of being unmarried and pregnant, the agony of deciding to give up the baby for adoption and the trauma of parting with her child. Most of this experience is concentrated in the space of a few months. The mother then has to live with the loss of her baby and the effects of this remain with her, one way or another, for the rest of her life. If the birth mother had received support and if she had been given the opportunity to talk about what had happened, then her long-term adjustment to the loss was likely to be good. However, the conditions that make adoption necessary are likely to mean that care, support and interest are not in plentiful supply. It is ironic that what the mother needs most from other people is least likely to be available, for it is the relative lack of these qualities in her close relationships that made the adoption necessary in the first place.

The way people adjust to loss is a well-understood process. When people grieve they follow a broadly recognizable sequence of reactions: shock and disbelief, anger and resentment, guilt, depression and withdrawal, and finally acceptance and resolution. But as we learned in Chapter 2, although the mother who relinquishes her child for adoption has many characteristics in common with others who have suffered a loss, there are special features peculiar to her situation that interfere with her ability to grieve in the normal way. Encouraged to 'forget the child' and 'get on with her life', the mother may fail to mourn her loss. The adoption remains as an unresolved grief which continues to disturb and distort her life so that she never reaches a stage when the loss is accepted. The fact that the child continues to exist, even though he or she has been 'lost', adds a confusing psychological twist to the grieving process. In contrast to other types of loss, many of the birth mother's feelings appear to intensify with time; her pain, anguish and anger may actually increase as the years go by. Feelings of guilt and self-blame continue unabated.

Living with loss is the theme of this chapter. The birth mother remains central to the story, but other familiar characters reappear and continue to play a key part in how the mother experiences her loss. What she thinks and feels affects and is affected by her relationship with her parents and the absent, adopted child. New people also enter the story: husbands, subsequent children, friends. The original script for the birth mother required her to 'disappear' and have the baby before 'reappearing', intact and apparently unchanged, either to carry on her life as if nothing had happened or to make a fresh start. The trauma of losing her baby was, to all intents and purposes, ignored or denied. Unfortunately, such a deep loss could not simply be forgotten. In many and complex ways, the failure to resolve the grief plagued new relationships and spawned fresh troubles and feelings of discomfort.

Chronologically, we shall follow the story through another four stages. One of the first things a birth mother has to consider when she begins to pick up the threads of her life is whether to tell anyone that she is a woman who has had a child and that the child was adopted. To tell or not to tell needs thought and management. The second stage finds the birth mother trying to live with her feelings of unresolved grief. For some, the loss is experienced as a constant dull background pain. For others, the feelings of loss remain dormant for long periods but occasionally surface when reminders are to hand or new setbacks are suffered. The third stage sees the mother move a few steps forward. Anger emerges, often directed at her parents, as she reviews the circumstances surrounding her pregnancy, the baby's birth and his or her adoption. The fourth stage in fact may overlap with the other three. The mother will find herself wondering about her adopted child. She may even want to meet her son or daughter. Her curiosity is aroused and she spends time and energy thinking about the lost infant.

NEW RELATIONSHIPS AND THE MANAGEMENT OF A SPOILED IDENTITY

The unmarried woman who found herself pregnant had the problem of how to manage an identity that was visibly spoiled and apparent to everyone she met. In Goffman's (1963) terms she was a 'discredited' person and her task was to conduct herself as best she could as a morally flawed individual. The mother who has surrendered her baby for adoption has a different problem. It may not be possible to tell by simply looking at her that she has had a baby outside marriage and that the child has been adopted. She has the potential to be discredited; she is therefore 'discreditable'. Whereas the discredited unmarried pregnant woman had the problem of managing tension in her social encounters, the birth mother who has given up her child has the task of *managing information* about her failing. 'To display or not to display; to tell or not to tell; to let on or not to let on; to lie or not to lie; and in each case, to whom, how, when and where' (ibid., p.57). For example, undressing in the presence of other people might pose major problems of concealment. A woman who was a nurse and had to change her clothes in order to work in the operating theatre was very conscious of her stretch marks and she would try to change out of the sight of her colleagues.

Stigma management is necessary for the birth mother as she is the subject of considerable opinion, prejudice and stereotyping. She needs to assume that many people will have views about the sort of woman who gets pregnant when she is not married and then places the child for adoption. The way such people react and treat the birth mother may be a product of those views. Therefore, in each new relationship, she has to decide whether or not to reveal the hidden aspects of her identity. Relationships generally require people to spend time together and the more time the birth mother spends with the other person the greater the chance of that person discovering the discreditable information. Relationships also oblige people to exchange intimate facts about self 'as evidence of trust and mutual commitment' (ibid., p.108). Thus, an element of anxiety is introduced every time the mother enters into a new, close relationship. On the other hand, for the other person not to know the true identity of the birth mother means that she feels that she is not truly known. If she does not reveal, then she lives a lie:

It's like a part of you that is not spoken about; it's there but nobody knows. I think, for a time, I found it really hard making new relationships and just talking to people. I felt like I was getting to know them but they weren't getting to know the real me. I was putting over just part of me. I found it hard to get on with people for a bit. I was OK with the people who knew everything. I felt safe with them. But new people didn't know me. It's almost like denying half of yourself in a way; it was so much a part of me.

Even on a day-to-day level, the birth mother finds herself vetting what is known about her. 'How many children do you have?' 'How old is your eldest?' 'Where did you have your first baby?' There are always two answers to questions such as these. But the urge is always to tell and very often the response to the disclosure becomes a test of that relationship. It applies both to men and women, though it seems to work particularly well on men. On learning of the adopted child the men who did not cope well with the revelation either ended the relationship or insisted that it was never mentioned again.

I went out with this Catholic doctor for a bit and it seemed like it was vaguely edging towards marriage. He had very high moral standards and when I told him of my past it threw him.

My husband – my ex-husband – he would never talk about the baby. I told him two weeks after I was going out with him, that I'd had a baby. He had to go away and think about whether he still wanted to go out with me or not; then he came back and said yes, he would still go out with me. The adoption though was starting to go wrong and so my daughter was put back into the nursery when she was three. This time I was about to get married and I went to see her and I was absolutely heartbroken. I just really wanted to have her back. He didn't want to know. He didn't want to tell his mother and we would never have a house with our own nice home and we would treat her differently to the other children, you know all this sort of thing, and I chose him. I've regretted it ever since.

The boyfriends and even my ex-husband just don't understand. They say, 'Nonsense. You should have got over all that years ago.' And that in a way, that's a real test of a relationship. If the man was unsympathetic then I knew the relationship was no good.

Other men accepted the adopted child's existence matter-of-factly. However, even that was not right for some mothers. They felt that the revelation deserved a more interested response! Nevertheless, many of the men who passed the test went on to marry the birth mother. This is how Janet met and assessed her husband:

I met him fairly soon after I arrived in Coventry. Actually, at the time he was going out with another woman I was friendly with, another Janet! He sort of, I don't know, he sort of symbolized lots of things I thought I'd missed out on. He was the opposite to my dad, which, as I said, was important to me. He and this Janet ceased their relationship because funnily enough she got pregnant by somebody else! Derek had a look in his diary and did a quick calculation, but it definitely wasn't his. It was quite important Janet getting pregnant. I felt desperately envious of her because she was pregnant and she was going to marry the father of the baby. And somehow, because she'd actually been in a sexual relationship with Derek there was some weird sort of connection between us which was illogical, but it was almost like she was having the baby I hadn't got, and I really felt green with envy . . . Not long after Janet and Tim decided to get married, Derek and I decided we'd get married – fifteen months after I'd had Emily. Derek was totally nonplussed, non-affected in the nicest possible way when I told him about her. Like 'Oh dear, that's sad, now let's get on and have some life together.' He had no moral position on it all, in that sense at all, which was great. I ended up marrying in a church, to a man with no faith but who did it for his mum. For me, it was buried even deeper. It was like now back full circle and I was the virgin that I should have been. It was a conscious thing to make myself what I should like to have been and I wanted other people to see me as . . .

. . . three months later I was pregnant again. I felt very happy. It was going to be perfect. It was going to be everything the other one should have been, and in lots of ways it was. It was very successful in terms of laying ghosts . . . the only slightly spoiling thing was that it was perfectly obvious to most people that she wasn't my first. And when she was born Derek was there and they congratulated him on his second child, which he took and handled remarkably well. I mean he really did. I admire him tremendously.

Patti (Shawyer, 1979, pp.125 and 147) mistook her boyfriend's initial reaction as lack of interest in what for her was an immensely important subject. 'When I first told him about the baby, we'd only been seeing each other for about two weeks and I thought, "He really means a lot to me and I'd like to get it right out in the open from the start. Because if he's going to reject me because of my past then I'd sooner he got it over and done with."' Patti had been rehearsing how she was going to tell the man she loved that she had had a baby. 'And I told him and he just sort of said, "Ho-hum", and moved on to the next subject. It didn't mean a thing to him.' But years later, she discovered what he had really thought. 'He could see at the time how upsetting it had been for me and sensed how much I feared rejection. His apparent uncon-cern was an effort to show me that he accepted my "past" and that it had no effect on our relationship. So we finally got that misunderstanding cleared up.'

Perhaps one of the most confusing relationships to have with a man is to marry the adopted child's father. Sandra, who was only fifteen when her daughter was born, returned home, left school and began a training course.

> Philip and I carried on seeing each other but it was very much on and off for a very long time. There was a stage when we were going to get married but I backed out. It seemed to go against the grain, because I felt if we were going to get married it seemed all wrong, like we should never have given her up if we were going to end up together. But I mean we couldn't have known that at the time. It was really hard. So then we left it for a few years.

Deykin *et al.* (1984) found that mothers who were married to the child's father were more likely than other mothers to regard the adoption as a 'negative influence on marriage' and report the following statement by one mother in evidence:

> My husband was the birth father and had made me feel guilty about the adoption. We could never talk about our daughter without feeling guilty and miserable. I felt so bad when I sent our children [subsequent births] to visit their grandparents in another state. I didn't want them to go but my husband insisted.

The problem of telling people who were not lovers generally proved easier to manage. The discreditable information could be either withheld or its consequences could be adjudged to be less significant. Rachel felt 'much, much older than many of her young women friends'. In fact she found making friends very hard. 'I still felt as if I had been immoral. I mean I really felt that I was not the same as the other girls of my age. I felt different, I felt older, like I had a vast experience that they hadn't and they couldn't understand, and I couldn't talk to them about it.' But on the whole, other women seemed a more reliable and safer repository for the confidence. It had taken Chris a while to learn this lesson: 'I'd started to be very careful who I talked to by now; only to women. I was amazed to discover that if I volunteered this information about myself that a lot of women would tell me very surprising things' (Inglis, 1984, p.126). Reciprocity and the sharing of feeling seemed more likely to occur between women than between men and women.

Although lovers and friends remain amongst the most significant new relationships in which information and identity have to be managed, there is one other type of new relationship that many mothers say is affected by their experience of having a baby adopted; being a mother to their other children. For many women there is the sheer joy and relief that they can have a child without shame. The child is the focus of much love, seeming to receive not only the affection warranted in his or her own right but also the feelings that could not be expended on the first child. In contrast, there are mothers who feel that they cannot love their second child while their first is still missing. It is as if the mother believes that it would not be fair on the adopted baby to enjoy the second child unreservedly. And yet a third reaction finds the birth mother afraid to invest too much love in her second child in case fate also removes that child from her. The pain of parting with another baby would be too much to bear and the only way to defend oneself against further hurt is not to become too involved. Taking this a stage further leads some women to conclude that they do not want any more children. They appear to have low self-esteem and believe themselves unworthy to have another child having failed the first: 'I always felt unfit to become a mother again (even though I loved children) after signing adoption papers. I have not been able to even hold a baby since the surrender' (Deykin *et al.*, 1984, p.277).

Often mothers imagined that to be married and pregnant must be a most wonderful state of affairs. When marriage and babies did transpire, the discrepancy between the ideal, understanding partner and the flesh-and-blood man they married was too great, and a final disillusionment took place. It was as if they could never be pregnant and happy. It was the loss of a dream.

Molly believed that her repeated pregnancies were partly explained by her 'chasing the lost baby'. With her second daughter, Susan, she had a difficult relationship. She was not the baby she had lost and Susan sensed this. 'She was rejecting me because I had rejected her when she was a baby' (ibid., p.66). Rockel and Ryburn (1988, pp.33–4) report mothers who said they went on having babies in an attempt to replace the missing one or that in their affections for later children they overcompensated, hoping to prove to themselves that they could be better mothers. One mother recalled that

> It took ages to bond with my next two babies ... it took me a while to realize that they weren't going away. And I had to go out to work – I couldn't just stay at home, because I got extremely depressed. And there was this feeling that I shouldn't really devote all my energies to these two, when I couldn't give any to the first one. It didn't seem fair.

UNRESOLVED GRIEF

According to Winkler and van Keppel (1984) the effects of relinquishing a child for adoption are negative and long-lasting. About half of the women they studied reported an increasing sense of loss over periods of up to thirty years. 'Even in my happiest moments,' reports one mother, 'there is an almost physical sense of loss; sometimes it is accompanied by a gnawing feeling in my abdomen halfway between discomfort and pain' (Roll *et al.*, 1986, p.264). In general, birth mothers had more problems of psychological adjustment compared to a matched group of women; the relinquishing mothers were more likely to suffer depression, anxiety and physical ill health. However, we need to remind ourselves that the researchers also found that not all women failed to adjust to the loss of their child. Women who had friends and relatives who were caring, thoughtful and understanding made better adjustments to their loss. The pain of relinquishment was still very much present, but they managed to grieve and eventually they found themselves on an even keel. 'I know if it hadn't been for my wonderful husband and family, I would not have been able to live with the fact that I had given up my baby. I can talk and cry about it with them' (Winkler and van Keppel, 1984, p.46). 'I am very lucky because I have a great mum that I can talk to – I've never had to bottle things up' (ibid., p.49). We also have to remind ourselves that most of the mothers mentioned in the literature are women who have experienced long-term difficulties adjusting to the loss of their child. The portraits are drawn to make a long overdue case, and although such women are probably in the majority, those who did attain peace of mind are under-represented in the birth mother's story.

Shawyer believes that birth mothers are women who suffer deeply from an unresolvable grief. 'Unresolvable, that is, until they meet their children again' (1979, p.xi). The birth mother's child is lost but not dead; her son or daughter continues to exist. This confuses her ability to grieve in any normal sense. The nagging knowledge that the child is with someone else, growing up, having birthdays, going to school, getting married and having children makes any adjustment to the loss both difficult and peculiar. The word used most often by mothers as they tell this part of their story is 'pain'. Many women speak of missing their child. And for a few, the pain becomes too much to bear and they 'go to pieces'.

Loss and Pain

The child is never forgotten but some mothers simply cannot stop thinking about their son or daughter. 'Never a day went by,' said one mother, 'for at least three or four years after he was born, when I didn't think of him. Every time I talked about him, tears came into my eyes' (Winkler and van Keppel, 1984, p.52). Until she discovered that she might be able to find out from the adoption agency how her twelve-year-old daughter was progressing, Pauline 'just kept thinking about her. I just couldn't get her out of my mind. I got so depressed with it.'

It seemed natural and inevitable to some women that their feelings of loss should stay with them for the rest of their lives. 'The feeling of loss has been strong for eighteen years – it was as though she died, only worse, she was out there somewhere,' was how a mother described her feeling (ibid., p.54). Although she felt she had begun to recover her equilibrium, another mother wrote, 'the feeling of a child conceived in my body will never disappear. The sorrow of a lost child and the mother crying out at night is imprinted on my heart' (Sorosky *et al.*, 1978, p.56). 'I think of her every day', 'I feel as though part of me is missing', and 'I've cried myself to sleep for almost twelve years over what happened' are typical of the intensity of feeling that mothers endure over many years (ibid., pp.57–9). And in the same batch of letters a woman who was sixteen when she had her daughter said of the adoption that 'It was the most painful thing I ever had to face. The feelings never really get resolved and go on.'

While some women hardly go a day without thinking of their child, others felt they had accepted the loss only to find that years later the feelings of unresolved grief returned, often with a vengeance. Twelve years ago a mother gave up her baby for adoption. She loved her baby and fought to keep her but failed. She was told that she would forget:

> For ten years after that I had pulled myself up by the bootstraps, when I succeeded to construct a good life for myself in which I gave and received love once more to my husband and son, when my life was set and secure, then I began to remember. And the memories were as clear as though they had been deep frozen and now were thawed. The memories floated mercilessly within my head, lacking order, priority and sequence.
>
> (ibid., p.57)

It is the pain that many birth mothers still feel that baffles them. If having the baby adopted was the most difficult decision the mothers felt they had ever had to make, the ensuing loss turned out to be the most painful experience of their lives. 'I have experienced many emotional and physical pains throughout my life,' wrote a mother, 'probably suffered more than most, but the most damaging was the adoption of my wee son when I was almost seventeen years old' (Shawyer, 1979, p.18). Twenty years later, not only did Nancy remember the pain and trauma of losing her baby, the pain remained: 'I still feel the hurt. I just can't get over what happened. It was the hardest and most painful thing that has ever happened to me and no one seems to understand.'

Not only is the child missed, but mothers say that a piece of themselves is missing. They talk of 'gaps' and 'holes' in their lives. They feel 'incomplete' or that bits of them are 'dead'. Christine wished she had kept her son

> because I miss him. I miss him physically. I miss him. When I first came out of hospital I felt like I had my arm chopped off or something, it was a physical missing him, and I miss him now. I mean my friend Veronica has a boy, Andrew, who is about the same age as James, and I enjoy his company but I am aware that James is not there. I sort of look for him. I feel if he traces me I'd have some peace at last, be a bit more complete.

Mixed up with the pain were feelings of guilt. In whichever direction she looked, the birth mother seemed to be at fault. She had become pregnant outside marriage and could not care for her baby. There was the nagging feeling that she had not done enough to prevent the loss. Cassie felt

> the most appalling guilt. That's a hard thing for me to cope with. The fact that I could give away my own child. I mean that's the worst thing you can do. But, well, it was a no-win situation. You know, it's just the most painful awful thing. Always the feeling of guilt.

> (Inglis, 1984, p.161)

Fay looked back on her past and wondered whether she should really have been able to cope and so keep her baby.

> I mean I was only seventeen, but you start to thinking whether perhaps you should have tried harder. I couldn't afford a flat, there were all kinds of obstacles. I just wouldn't have been able to

cope, but you do wonder whether you might just have managed. And so you're left with a heck of a lot of guilt. I've survived other things and so you think, 'If I'd kept her, I would have survived that.'

Triggering the Feelings of Loss

Although most mothers coped with life on a day-to-day level, there would be times when the memories and the pain would return. An event would trigger the old feelings of loss. Some triggers could be anticipated: birthdays and places would revive familiar pains and heartaches. Others would come out of the blue: the birth of a second child or the death of a friend's baby.

Not surprisingly birthdays were the most frequent and often most potent reminders of the hurt: 'While I have no regrets over the adoption, feeling it was the right thing to do then, and I still do, her birthday each year comes round, still making me feel sad and wondering how life is treating her.' 'I always sit and cry when his birthday comes round' (Shawyer, 1979, pp.103 and 166). For Louise, birthdays were a 'sickening' time. 'It's as if there's a time-clock that clicks on around then whatever I think' (Inglis, 1984, p.143). The only way Mary could cope with her daughter's birthday was to go away two days before the anniversary: 'My husband used to keep away from me. I used to clear off to a friend's house and cry buckets ... my family used to dread July. They couldn't live with me.'

Getting pregnant and giving birth to a second child could also act as a powerful reminder of the first baby. Different mothers reacted differently to the second pregnancy. As we have heard, many mothers savoured the freedom to enjoy and luxuriate in a wanted and accepted pregnancy. It was as if they were going to make up for all the deficiencies of the first birth. However, there were other mothers who felt guilty about enjoying their second pregnancy. The memories of the first baby interfered with the ability to relax and appreciate the later birth. All the suppressed pain of the earlier loss would surface as the mother repeated each stage of having a baby. 'It was not until the birth of my second child, also a boy, that I was overcome by the vast sense of loss associated with my first baby' (Winkler and van Keppel, 1984, p.53). When her daughter was born, Marianne could not help but compare the fuss that people made of her and the baby with the silence and neglect that she and her first daughter had experienced: 'I held my second baby and thought of my first. Poor little mite. It seemed as if only me had loved her and everyone else didn't want to know. I sat there holding Michelle and cried, cried for Lisa.'

Sandra's second and third children both reminded her of the first child:

> When Thomas was born it really brought it all back again really strongly. Every time he did something, I'd think about her and think I'd missed it all ... I've thought about her an awful lot on and off, obviously some times more than others. Birthdays. Like when people say how many children have you got, and things like that, and little things, like writing out Lucy's birth book, you know the books you have after they are born. It's got a page for brothers and sisters and I'm tempted to put down Karen, because they are brothers and sisters you know because we are married now, they are full brothers and sisters. But I didn't put her name in. It's like a secret in a way.

The other type of event that was likely to trigger old feelings of loss were those occasions when the birth mother suffered a further loss, sometimes minor, but sufficient to revive the unresolved grief associated with the original loss. It seems to the mother and others that she is overreacting to the new loss, but in reality what the birth mother is experiencing is a reawakening of all the feelings of grief and sadness surrounding the earlier loss. Many years later, Janet was unlucky enough to suffer a whole series of upsets and setbacks which bothered her considerably. Her son told her he was gay, it was thought that her daughter might have skin cancer and a close friend died. It was only during a talk with a counsellor, in which she cried a great deal, that she realized that she was handling all kinds of loss:

> my adopted child, the potential loss of my daughter, the lost expectations of my only son ... and my friend Maggie, of course. I discovered she died of a brain tumour and two days before she

died she had a Caesarean section and there was a twenty-eight-week-old baby, who was in hospital . . . I went to see this baby and I wanted to bring him out. He just got completely confused in my mind with who he was. I thought, 'I can't leave him in hospital, I've got to take him home' . . . So there was this real load of losses and babies and things all happening one after the other.

In Pain and Needing Help

The mothers who were adjusting least well often became depressed and even psychiatrically ill. These women said they could not sleep, they cried a lot, and felt as if they were 'going to pieces' or 'going crazy'. Some sought the help of a psychotherapist or a professional counsellor. Lorraine explained that she had repressed all the things that had happened to her when she was sixteen: 'it was the only way I could deal with giving my daughter away; not to think about it'. Lorraine's adopted daughter is now a young woman and a year ago she telephoned her mother, who was out at the time. The call was not repeated and after that time Lorraine suffered a very bad year:

I felt I couldn't cope, I didn't go to work. I was breaking down. I wasn't sleeping. I've become an insomniac. I couldn't work. I was taking weeks off. I was having tablets but they were doing no good. I was a nervous wreck. And it's not me, you see. I am this sort of big-mouth jolly person who gets on with things – let's do it now, let's get on with it. And all of a sudden, I wasn't there, I wasn't coping . . . I just wanted to cut myself off, become completely withdrawn . . . I'm going to a psychologist for treatment, well, not treatment; he listens to me, he talks to me, and that helps enormously.

Those most prone to a breakdown seemed to have thrown themselves into work or new relationships with great energy and determination. They refused to think about the child and vigorously 'got on with their life', but at breakneck speed. The end result was some kind of relapse or mental breakdown. Once having stopped, these mothers joined others who had never managed to climb out of their despair and who had remained in some kind of depressed state from the time of the baby's relinquishment. Self-esteem is low amongst this group; many women see themselves as worthless and of no value or interest. They expect to be punished both for having a baby and for placing the child for adoption. There is talk of suicide, there are feelings of depression and there is much crying. Twenty-three years after her baby's birth, Kate went into a deep depression which she believed to be 'a kind of grieving period I didn't go through all those years ago'. This belated response to the child's loss was not uncommon. Lucy's story captures many of the difficulties and problems experienced by this group. She was eighteen when she gave birth to her son. For several months she struggled to look after him, but with little money and no support it became increasingly difficult for her to cope. After a private fostering arrangement broke down, Liam was received into the care of the local authority when he was barely six months old. A short spell in a nursery was followed by his transfer to foster parents who eventually adopted him, though Lucy never gave her consent. Her life over the last twenty-one years has not been easy:

> For most of that time I never really acknowledged Liam and the adoption and that I'd lost my child. I was trying to keep the lid on it. And really I couldn't . . . There was a time when I completely crumbled. I've had really bad depression and there have been times when I've drunk heavily . . . I've had psychiatric help and pills, but looking back I now see that I did what everyone told me to do. I didn't have the strength to make any decisions myself . . . I've been let down by my so-called family. When my mother eventually learned about Liam all she said was 'Who've you told about this baby? You're not to tell anyone.' I always held this against her to the day she died. I'm not bitter now. I'm angry.

PARENTS, BETRAYAL AND ANGER

Perhaps one of the first signs of emotional progress along the road to recovery and adjustment is the expression of anger. Not all birth mothers display anger or feel outraged. Many women continue to feel that they were solely responsible for what happened to their child. Guilt is their lot. It is often difficult to be angry when what you feel angry about is surrounded by feelings of shame and guilt. The right to be angry only emerges once the mother stops blaming herself. If our suspicion is correct that adoption and the experiences that surround it are to a large extent constructed by people who are important to the birth mother, it might be expected that much of her anger, if targeted accurately, will be aimed at her parents, and indeed this often seems to be the case. But the birth mother also blames herself and much of her anger is self-directed. She blames herself for being weak and not standing up to people. She feels, not always realistically, that if she had been stronger and more assertive, the baby would never have been adopted.

The most primitive and perhaps least constructive response of the angry mother is to wreak revenge. The birth mother resents her own mother or the child's father for bringing her so much pain and suffering:

I was angry at them for making me give the baby up, and in some ways I enjoyed not having another one. I hate to admit that, but I did. I could see their guilt over it, and I could think, 'Now *they're* suffering. I've suffered for years and now I'm watching their faces.'

(Rockel and Ryburn, 1988, pp.32–3)

Parents who insisted on adoption as the best course of action and failed to bring their daughter into the decision-making process were not always recognized as the true instigators of adoption at the time. Only with the passing of the years does the birth mother begin to piece together the conversations and suggestions that took place during her pregnancy and after the birth. She was weak and they were strong. Their will prevailed but the pain was hers and for this she may not forgive them. She directs her growing anger at what they did to her and the baby. 'I had a lot of jolting experiences,' recalled Jeanette. 'My mother would some-times take a swipe at me and rub it in. The irresponsibility of my mother started to dawn. We were having words about something and I was crying and I said, "You've ruined my life, you stupid bitch"' (Inglis, 1984, p.99). In a similar way, it dawned on

Lorraine that her father was the insidious force behind the decision to have her baby adopted, though she did not recognize it at the time:

I am now at the stage where I don't think my father was very considerate of me. This is a very hard thing for me to say because my dad was a very loving, caring man ... he's dead now and maybe that's lucky because I would be very angry and so he's gone before I can show him that and in many ways I'm glad because in many ways I don't think I'd be able to control my feelings. I always believed that he'd done it for me, but now I'm in the psychotherapy I'm beginning to feel that he didn't; that he really did it because he just couldn't bear the shame ... If he had simply said he couldn't cope with public opinion or something but what he did say was 'You'll have no life of your own. If you give this one away, you'll get married, you'll be happy, you'll have other children.' Well it's not true. You can have other children but you can't replace the one you've lost. All I then wanted to do was get married and have children, because I thought that it would sort of fill the space. It hasn't. The marriage isn't incredibly happy ... It would have been better for me to have fought ... I should have said, 'Sod you all.' I should have done that and said, 'This is my baby. I'm not going to give my baby away. You can go to hell, I am keeping my baby.'

Mary was pleased with her mounting anger. Over the space of eighteen years she saw herself change from 'wimp' to 'a very strong person' and with that strength her anger grew. She blames her mother for wrenching her baby daughter from her care. Mary was not consulted. It was all planned 'behind my back' and a few weeks after the baby was born it was taken to America by a relative who already had an adopted son:

I feel very used, you know, very worthless. My family didn't help me any, you know, and that's why I feel so bitter about everything ... My mother was a strong person, a very hard person. Nobody knew my feelings or how I felt about the baby. I just kept quiet ... Looking back I think I had a very raw deal ... Well the woman who was a relative of my mother came over and then was joined by her husband and he brought their adopted son over . . . and they decided to have a party, a farewell thing, before they went back home. Well I couldn't handle it. I was outside, I was so upset and she came round and she said, 'You'll get married and have your own, you've got a wonderful man there' . . . and I remember getting very angry with her and I said, 'You'll never get away with this, you'll never,' I said. 'You know I want that child and you're taking her out of the country' . . . and now she's terrified. I'll find her wherever she goes . . . I think the only way to get my own back is to stay angry, because if I don't stay angry I'm not going to do anything about it . . . As far as I'm concerned that child was stolen. I don't care whether it was done legally, she was still stolen . . . I'm angry with my mother and I'm angry with myself.

Slightly more sophisticated anger appears when the birth mother is able to recognize that she was 'sold a line', that she was 'conned' into having the baby adopted 'for the child's own good' or 'the birth mother's own good', when all along it was the parents who were going to benefit in some way. Olga was a staunch Christian. Her pregnancy was viewed as a sin and the only way to expiate the sin was to have the child adopted. 'And now I'm really, really angry about that. I was conned into adoption because of Christian principles.'

Rather than accept that they were to blame for the outcome, these mothers now thought that the people and the situation in which they found themselves at the time were more at fault. They had been betrayed. As young women they were not really 'sinful' or 'immoral', just 'unlucky'. All the guilt and the hurt they had been made to suffer as a result of that bad luck now seemed unfair. Being sinful and immoral, the mothers were told, they had no right to enjoy their baby; wrongdoing was not to be rewarded with pleasure. If the women had maternal feelings, they had to be repressed as not the kind of thing that an unmarried mother should feel and certainly not the type of emotion an illegitimate child should expect to receive. The baby had to go to a home where the couple were married and all these pleasurable sensations could have legitimate expression. 'Looking back I can't believe how I went along with all the bullshit,' fumed Pat:

I'd had a child and wasn't married and so I couldn't be a mother and do all the motherly things like cuddle my baby and love my baby, because that would not be right and here's the catch: because I couldn't do all these motherly things because I shouldn't, then someone else should because they could, because they were allowed to because they were married. So that was why the baby had to be adopted. Because she needed a mother and I couldn't be a mother because of the way I'd got pregnant and not being married. Bloody ironic, don't you think? Too bloody clever when you're only seventeen. That's how my mother put it, not in those words, but that's what it boiled down to and I'm so angry with her, for betraying me and my child – her own, her first grand-daughter!

WONDERING ABOUT THE LOST CHILD

Conventionally, the inclination to search for the lost person occurs early in a person's reaction to grief. The bereaved often 'see' their loved one or 'hear' their voice. But the birth mother's loss is not entirely normal. Her child still exists, but she may have no tangible evidence of the baby at all. Her friends may not have seen the baby, may not even know about him or her. The baby has no belongings, there is no grave, no focus of grief. Enid kept a snapshot of her baby. 'I used to get it out and cry. In the end I got rid of it because I was frightened my children would see it and ask who it was. I was really silly. I could easily have made up something. I suppose it shows how ashamed I was. I then had nothing left of my son.' Once more Enid cried for the child whom she gave up thirty years ago. The prospect of recovering the child is not altogether fanciful, particularly as the child approaches adulthood and he or she might think of searching for the birth mother. The mother who talks about her lost child many years after the adoption does so in a reflective, wistful fashion. She has lived with the loss for a long time and although her feelings of grief remain unresolved they are less likely to have the desperate quality that characterized the first few months of life without the baby.

Towards the end of her story, the mother returns to thinking about the child. She has exhausted her accounts of how she has fared in life, she has said all she can say about her parents, her relationships with husbands, lovers and friends. Her final thoughts are about the child she lost. She is inclined to *wonder* about him or her, *imagine* what he or she is like. There are moments in the day when she may *daydream* about the child, *curious* about where he is or what she is doing. 'I only wish to know if the child is alive and well. I have wondered about her all these years . . .' (Sorosky *et al.*, 1978, p.65). Typically, the birth mother is keen to state that she is happily married and has other children that she loves, but there is an aching need to know about her first child. 'I have three fine, healthy children now, but very rarely go through a day without wondering and longing to know what has happened to her.'

Often, though increasingly less so, the last time the mother saw her child was as a baby. As the years go by she tries to imagine how the child is progressing, what clothes she might like, what interests he may have. 'I had some friends round the corner,' reflected Sandra, 'and they had a little girl the same age as Julie so I didn't think of her as a baby. I used to look at their girl and think "Oh, she's like that now. I wonder if she's wearing those funny socks, if she's very trendy, what if she's stealing her father's jumpers to wear as they do now."' Imagining what a daughter might wear was also a theme in Wendy's concluding thoughts as she tried to picture her child as a growing adolescent:

Hardly a day goes by without me thinking of my baby. I mean, I don't actually picture her as a baby any more, but each birthday I just try to picture her a year older. Now I've even pictured her as a completely freaked-out punk wearing leather and chains! I think maybe she's developed artistic things. She could be going to college like her father, or she might have turned musical or she might not be like any of us at all, but I try to imagine what she looks like.

In their heart of hearts not a few mothers confess that what they would really like to do is meet their grown-up child, or if this was not possible, then at least see them at a distance or be given a photograph. 'I pray that one day my son and I will meet,' wrote one mother. Another said that she had a son twenty years ago when she was seventeen and that because of her circumstances she was pressured into having him adopted: 'I have never stopped wondering about him and have often cried myself to sleep over letting him go ... I would dearly love to see him. However if that's not possible, I would be satisfied with a photo and news of how he is getting on' (Shawyer, 1979, pp.110 and 118). In lieu of an actual meeting, some mothers contented themselves with imagining what the meeting would be like. 'Sometimes I have this daydream,' admitted Leonie, 'that one day I'll get a letter and this lovely girl will turn up and I'll explain it all and she'll forgive me and then it will be over. I don't go any further than that. It's only a fantasy and you can't let that develop too much' (Inglis, 1984, p.169). Leonie was suitably cautious in letting her hopes build up. This was not the case for one of the mothers quoted by Deykin *et al.*: 'I have become obsessed with finding her. I've lost a lot of sleep and have headaches all the time. I think about her every minute of the day' (1984, p.276).

In spite of their compelling desire to hear about or meet their child, the majority of mothers were acutely aware of how threatening this might be for both the child and the adopters. They spoke of not wishing to 'disturb' or 'interfere' with the child's life; they went to considerable pains to explain that they had no intention of upsetting anyone. Such birth mothers said that ideally they would just like to see their son or daughter, unbeknown to the child, and then they might leave reassured and satisfied. In a letter a mother explained how she placed her daughter for adoption seven years ago. The birth mother is now 'extremely happily married' to an understanding husband who knows all about her past. She has two more children of her 'own' but would still like to know how her first child is growing up:

> Please don't misunderstand, that we would upset anyone in any way. I know that she is probably very happy and loves her parents as her own, and I never would dream of taking the matter any further and identifying myself to her or anyone concerned, but I suppose it's just curiosity where she is and what she looks like, etc. We would be quite happy if we could perhaps discreetly glimpse her or her present home and leave it at that. I find myself looking at my other two children and just wondering.
>
> (Shawyer, 1979, p.92)

The least compromising women in this group would like not only to meet the child but take the child back. 'Six years ago, I gave my son up for adoption, which was the last thing I wanted. I would do anything to have my son back. I have never got over giving him away . . .' Louise in fact did not want to disrupt her son's life, but then made the following admission: 'It's apparently not the thing to do to want to steal them back, but underneath, of course, you must admit you would if you could' (ibid., pp.101 and 163).

A small number of mothers had heard news of their child or even seen a photograph of him or her. It seemed to help. Real knowledge filled the gap; it helped replace what was felt to be missing. 'I *have* felt empty – there has been this emptiness inside of me since she went. A part of me had gone. And now that I have this information, that part's back and I feel more complete and whole again. I feel more confident. I've got my self-esteem.' Rockel and Ryburn (1988, p.165) give this example and others as evidence that to know how things are turning out is reassuring to the birth mother. Such evidence, they argue, provides strong support for the idea of open adoptions in which the birth mother is kept in the picture and can more easily adjust to and eventually accept the need for and the benefits of the adoption. Only after twelve years of wondering and thinking about her daughter did Sandra hear any news of her child. She approached the adoption agency who eventually furnished her with news about Karen. And to Sandra's delight the agency also asked her to provide information for their files in case Karen might want to find out more about Sandra and her husband:

I feel more relaxed now. I was getting really depressed just thinking about her. I couldn't get her out of my mind. You really felt you had no rights whatsoever to any information, which was horrible. I still hope that she will get in touch. I would really love to see her, I suppose. Anyway, that's up to her. But I do feel more settled in my mind now that I know something of how she is.

But although most stories reveal the mother imagining a happy ending in which she is reunited with her child, it must be noted that there are a small number of women who definitely do not want to meet or be confronted with their adopted child. A few mothers actively dread this prospect. There is the fear that their lives will be disrupted, if not destroyed, by their child's unwelcome return. Unlike the mothers who do want to see their son or daughter, women in this group have not told anybody that they are a birth mother, least of all husbands and children. They are a minority, but their feelings are vividly caught in a batch of letters received by Sorosky *et al.* (1978, pp.70–71). These mothers, although not necessarily denying that they might be curious about their son or daughter, nevertheless claim to be detached from the child. They do not feel like nor do they wish to be a mother to the child they relinquished many years ago:

> I am distressed that so many women who have managed to build a new life for themselves may now have them shattered again by this stupid move to open birth records to adopted children. If there are some women who wish to live in the past then they should be permitted to do so. I learned from my mistake and do not wish to have it thrown in my face now or ever.

> I had an illegitimate child when I was nineteen. No one knew about it except my parents. Three years later I got married. My husband has no idea of my past nor will he be told. I now have a prestigious job, a child and a lovely home. I am now thirty years of age. I am afraid that if the child ever came to my front door it would be the end of my marriage. My husband would probably get custody of our child.

However, if Shawyer (1979) is to be believed, the only way for a birth mother to finally resolve her feelings of grief is to be reunited with her child, or at least to meet and know the child as a real person. The child would then no longer be experienced as a 'missing' part of the mother. Deykin *et al.* (1984) studied 334 'surrendering' parents. The parents were asked if they had ever considered searching for their lost child. The vast majority (96 per cent) said they had contemplated looking for their child, while 65 per cent indicated that they had actually initiated a search (p. 274). It also emerged that birth parents who said that the adoption was the result of pressure from other people (family, social workers, health workers) were significantly more likely to search than those who chose adoption for personal reasons (youth or a desire to finish school). Time was also an important factor. 'Parents who had surrendered children more than twelve years ago were more likely to have searched than those who surrendered children more recently' (ibid., pp.274–5).

The birth mother's story generally closes with the hope that one day she will see her child again, not just to see them and to touch them but to explain – explain why she chose adoption, explain that they were loved, explain that not for one moment had she ever forgotten them. In seeing them, they will also see her, see that she is not a disreputable woman or a 'slut', that they might be proud of her, that she has 'amounted to something'.

Patti was quite clear that she wanted her daughter to know 'how much I love her. That's something I really need to do' (Shawyer, 1979, p.144). More than anything Louise wanted to give her son a big hug and 'tell him why I gave him away, so he won't think it was because I didn't love him' (ibid., p.166). Thoughts that the child might grow up believing she had carelessly abandoned her baby could torment the mother. 'I gave up a boy for adoption eight years ago,' explained a mother. 'The past years have been pure hell for me. Does that little boy think I deserted him, that I didn't love him? That I never think of him or that I don't wonder what he does on his birthdays and Christmas?' (Sorosky et al., 1978, p.61). For the mother, the great attraction of meeting with the lost child is the opportunity it provides to right so many possible wrongs. She feels she may be made whole again, she can explain what really happened. She can announce her love and she can establish her worth. Made complete, she can pick up the threads of her life again. These hopes may not always be realized or even realistic, but they make sense to the birth mother.

6
Finding a Voice

Why have mothers who have had a child adopted remained silent and invisible for so long? Why now are they finding a voice and speaking out?

Historically, birth mothers have neither looked for nor received social recognition or acknowledgement. It was as though the thousands of adopted children were not connected to a birth mother. When adoptive parents received the baby, it seemed to come from the adoption agency or the social worker. Indeed, the telephone call often began with the joyful news, '*We* have a baby for you.' It was, in the words of Suzanne Arms, an 'immaculate deception'. The birth mother was described to the adoptive parents in general, rather stereotyped terms: 'she was a student nurse and quite musical'; or 'she worked in a hotel and was a very practical sort of girl'. This was quite deliberate. It was felt best that the adoptive parents did not picture the mother as a 'real person' because it might interfere with the process of bonding between them and the baby. Some adoption agencies discouraged birth mothers from buying gifts for the baby because the child would now have everything he needed. Tangible signs of the birth mother's existence were to be avoided. It was also equally true that birth mothers were told little about the people who were to become the adoptive parents, except how much the couple longed for a child and the wonderful home that they could offer. This was intended as comfort and reassurance for the mother that she was doing the right thing in having her child adopted. After parting with her child, she was advised to look forward and to avoid reminders of her baby.

THE FRAGILE INSTITUTION

In order to understand the birth mother's silence about her experience, it is necessary to consider how adoption is defined and how her role was prescribed. Adoption was, and is, highly prized as a way of caring for children who cannot be brought up by the parents to whom they were born. The Curtis Committee Report which preceded the 1948 Children Act called it 'the most completely satisfactory method of providing a substitute home'. Nearly thirty years later it was termed 'the best form of substitute care yet devised for children whose parents could not care for them' (Kellmer-Pringle, 1972).

More recently, there has been a quest to achieve stability and permanence for children who are living with foster parents and again adoption has been seen as the surest way of providing this.

The 'flip side' of adoption, however, includes features which immediately seem problematic as a way of organizing human relationships. Adoption is an inflexible instrument defined partly in law and partly by the policies and regulations of adoption agencies. Those involved have to fit in. Adopters seeking a child need to make themselves acceptable to the agency, or else they may not be approved as adopters. For the birth mother, the adoption agency promised a good home for the child she was unable to keep. She was told that her child would have two parents and be free from the stigma of illegitimacy. The child would have everything he needed materially. Her part in the arrangement was to hand over her baby in the knowledge she might never hear any news of the child for the rest of her life, and to sign consent to adoption. If an agency placed the child, the adoptive parents were identified only by a number. In the words of the judge in an adoption case, an adoption order provides 'a veil between the past and the present lives of adopted persons and makes it as opaque and impenetrable as possible: like the veil which God has placed between the living and the dead' (*Lawson* v. *Registrar General*, 106 *LJ* 204, 1956).

The birth mother was told that the 'impenetrable veil' protected her and kept her secret safe. It also meant that she could not act on an impulse to try to find her child. A survey conducted in Canada revealed that 77 per cent of a group of birth mothers admitted to having 'very frequently' or 'somewhat frequently' thought of a child they had surrendered fourteen years previously (Sachdev, 1989). The inclination to stay in touch with the child and seek assurance that he was well had had to be suppressed. The curiosity that the adopted child may feel in the future about his origins would remain unsatisfied. Secrecy and concealment are the hallmarks of adoption and were seen as essential to preserve its integrity.

BARRIERS TO OVERCOME

As we have seen, a birth mother was in no doubt that she had offended society's rules. She had probably been warned – most girls were – that to become pregnant and have an illegitimate child was the worst thing that could happen. Few 'crimes' were so anticipated and the consequences spelled out in advance: 'don't expect to bring a baby home, it would break your father's heart'.

Ironically, young women were also urged to make themselves attractive to men and given advice on how to achieve this. Romantic fiction in women's magazines contained descriptions of beautiful women going 'limp in the arms' of a strong man, powerless to resist his will. In a society which was so condemning of unmarried motherhood, it would have been less confusing for women if they had been told how they could combine attracting a man, being overcome by his ardour and remaining a virgin.

A woman who was pregnant and unmarried was easily persuaded that she lacked the essential qualifications to be a mother. She already felt foolish for being in her predicament. She had made a mess of her life. She had trusted someone who proved untrustworthy or just gambled and lost. The most that she could hope for was the chance to put her 'mistake' behind her once the baby was born. As one mother said, 'I was told it was for the best, and if I loved him enough, I would give him up. I made myself believe it.'

For a mother to rebel, once she had agreed to adoption, meant causing her family anxiety and incurring the displeasure of a social worker on whom she had learned to depend. Adoption social workers often felt strongly that they had 'failed' if a mother elected to take the perilous path of single parenthood. She knew that she lacked the material and social support to keep her child. Furthermore she was taking away a baby from parents who had waited and longed for a child. She was being selfish when she could offer her child so little. It was assumed, especially if the birth mother was a teenager, that she would soon forget her child. One mother was sent on a skiing holiday and when she returned with snapshots showing her smiling, her own mother said with relief, 'I knew you didn't really want that baby.'

OUT OF THE SHADOWS

Many birth mothers have disclosed their secret in the context of a personal relationship, but few have spoken publicly about their experience. This is slowly changing. Recently there have been magazine articles about women who have relinquished a child for adoption. The birth mother now features when adoption is discussed, and she is acknowledged as a member of the 'adoption triangle' with the adopted child and the adoptive parents. She appears in television soap operas. All this would have been unthinkable only a few years ago.

A number of factors have made it possible, if not easy, for birth mothers to speak about their experience. The most obvious of these is the change in attitude and greater social acceptance of sexual relationships outside marriage. Mothers bringing up children on their own are now all 'single' mothers, whether separated, divorced, widowed or unmarried. Couples who are living together announce the birth of a baby in the same way as those who are married. In these changed times, the revelation that a woman gave birth to a child before marriage is scarcely shocking. It is much more difficult to explain why the baby was adopted. It would be hard for a young woman in the 1990s to imagine the scale of family crisis precipitated by an illegitimate pregnancy in the 1950s and 1960s. It is also difficult for a birth mother to recapture the pressures that were on her at the time of her baby's birth. One mother spoke of her feeling that if only she had simply refused to sign the consent papers, the adoption could not have gone ahead. She was in her late thirties at the time she was interviewed, but only sixteen when her daughter was born. A single woman who brings up a child today may be applauded as independent and strong; the stigma has passed from the unwed mother to the mother who relinquishes her child.

THE VOICE OF THE CHILD

The greater social acceptance of motherhood outside marriage has paradoxically left the birth mother with more knots to untie.

She gave up her child because she was unmarried and now this is considered a slight reason for doing so. Changing moral standards alone would not have been sufficient to persuade the birth mother to claim her role. Much more powerful has been the voice of the adopted child. Adopted people were granted the right to obtain their original birth certificates when they became eighteen in the Children Act 1975. This legislation was contentious because it changed the rules for everyone concerned with adoption. Many people were concerned that a birth mother might have her new life destroyed by the reappearance of a child relinquished long ago, but the right of the adopted child to knowledge about his birth parents was seen as carrying greater weight than any possible upset in her life.

Prior to 1975 only Scotland and Finland allowed adopted adults automatic access to their birth records. Surprisingly few adopted people in these countries took advantage of their right to discover their parentage; between the years 1961 and 1970 an average of forty-two people (or 1.5 per thousand of adopted people over seventeen years old) did so in Scotland. John Trise-liotis (1973) interviewed seventy people who had applied for their birth details and concluded that while many of those in his sample had not been happily adopted, and some were seeking a birth mother soon after the loss of an adoptive parent, adopted people 'need to know as much as possible about the circumstances of their adoption and about their genealogical background in order to integrate these facts into their developing personality'. The idea that it is normal, to be expected and encouraged, for adopted people to seek information about themselves has gradually gained ground. Florence Fisher (1973) and Betty Jean Lifton (1979) have both written compelling accounts of their experience as adopted people and argue that it is a basic human right to have access to information about birth parentage. The notion that curiosity about one's background is either an indication of psychological disturbance or a sign that the adoption did not 'take' is losing credit and there is now a continuous, if fluctuating, flow of inquiries. (In 1983 2,745 people applied for information.)

All birth mothers know that some adopted people try to estab-lish a link with a birth parent. After a lifetime of trying to manage her feelings, the birth mother hears that her child wants to know her. She anticipated rejection and anger, but instead finds a longing that resonates with her own.

Some birth mothers feel that they should have the legal right to search for their children, others consider that the initiative should always remain with the child: 'I don't feel I've any right to look for my daughter. I gave her up, I have to live with that. I just wait and hope that she wants to find me.'

All birth mothers are aware that they could be found by their children, and this fact alone changes the bargain that was struck when their babies were relinquished for adoption.

The possibility of reunion between birth mother and child throws into sharp relief the most difficult issues posed by adoption – issues which could be avoided but not resolved when an adoption order meant wiping out a child's history prior to that legal event. One of the most contentious is who qualifies as the 'real' mother? Adoptive parents feel vulnerable, and an anonymous correspondent to a newspaper in response to a feature on reunions between birth relatives wrote, 'Why . . . is there never any mention of the "real" parents? The ones who have loved, nurtured and comforted their child nearly every day of their lives?' (*Guardian*, 4 July 1990). The birth mothers are in no doubt about the answer to this question. They know that the adoptive mother is the real mother. The birth mother does not seek this status. As one mother said, 'I don't want him to be a son . . . I'm not going to grab him and dress him in swaddling clothes; I just want to answer his questions and tell him that it wasn't because I didn't want him that he was adopted.'

WOMEN'S VOICES

During the past two decades the feminist movement has had a marked effect on the way women think about their lives. This is the case whether or not a woman considers herself to be a feminist and irrespective of any obvious change or gains in her life. Women have become more aware of their unequal position in society and, like it or not, their consciousness has been raised.

There has been a similar shift in the way women are portrayed in the serious press and on television. Women now have the chance to see their own reflection, and it has become crystal clear that their second-class status in legal and economic terms is duplicated in the sphere of personal and sexual relationships. Women have defined violence against them as a problem of grave social concern and have drawn attention to the inadequacy of established psychological theory to explain behaviour such as rape and wife-battering.

In this questioning climate, birth mothers, along with other women, have begun to reassess their lives. The promise made to the mother who relinquished her child that she could put the event of the baby's birth behind her proved false. Her sense of loss has not diminished with time, and her relationship with her family, particularly her own mother, is tarnished. Many birth mothers express anger at their mothers for failing them when they were most in need. It seems as though one generation of women always has great difficulty in standing in the shoes of another.

The mother who reflects on her decision to surrender her child becomes aware of the strength of the forces which pushed her in that direction. She finds herself more angry but less guilty. She also realizes that her 'crime', the conception of an out-of-wedlock child, has shrunk to a commonplace event.

Birth mothers have not become a 'cause' among feminists. In spite of their vast numbers, their experiences remained personal and private, their stories untold. As a group they have failed to gain an identity; as individuals they have escaped notice. Mothers would rarely disclose that they had lost a child to adoption. Marianne, who relinquished her son for adoption twenty-five years ago, recalls the amazement that she and another woman felt when they revealed to each other that they were birth mothers after fifteen years of a very close friendship. Individual experiences remained discrete. Birth mothers have not appeared in the pages of those who write so strongly and eloquently about women's lives. It is as if the birth mother's dilemma confuses those who wish to think clearly and consistently about women and their relationship to children and motherhood. The absence of the birth mother in feminist literature hints at the difficulty that women have in treading a steady and uncluttered path through matters of reproduction.

The issue of motherhood, it seems, is a minefield in feminist debate. It divides women as much as it unites them. The radical feminist sees motherhood as a political issue. The only hope for women to escape their oppression is for them to fight against the idea that having children is a part of their natural destiny. They cannot begin to be free until they recognize that a woman's wish for a child is a response to men's desire that women produce children. At the heart of this debate is the tension between women having babies and women being the prime carers of children. Producing children should not mean that you have to rear them. In contrast, feminists in the liberal camp often find themselves arguing for the right of some women to have babies. They talk for those who want to become mothers who previously have been dismissed as unfit. Why shouldn't single mothers have babies; who says that lesbians should not be allowed to bring up their own children? In demanding the rights of women, liberal feminists logically find themselves supporting those who want babies outside the narrow boundaries drawn by men.

But as much as motherhood can divide women, it has the power to unite them – across class, across race, across age. Having a baby and being a mother are experiences that can be shared. It brings women together wherever and whenever they meet. However, at least not until recently, the woman who had her baby adopted could not share such experiences. She denied being a mother, she could not join in the common pleasure. This is beginning to change, slowly but surely. Only now are women learning to acknowledge that they are mothers who have given up a child for adoption. They now have the chance to find their sisters who, like them, have experienced the peculiar emotions that surround giving up a baby to another woman. Their feelings range from wondering if they have ever really been a mother at all to recognizing that their experiences of motherhood are of a unique and particularly painful kind. For mothers who do meet and tell their stories, the unifying forces at work are great, for not only can their motherhood now be shared, they can also speak about that which for so long could not be spoken. Their unique and particularly painful experience of motherhood brings them closer together. They have much more than simple parenthood in common. As we shall hear in the following chapters, for the birth mother who wishes to speak out, at long last there are receptive ears and the possibility of meeting others who, like them, are struggling to reclaim their full identity as a mother who has given up a baby for adoption.

7
A Helping Hand, a Listening Ear

Having looked closely at the position of women who have parted with a child for adoption, at their circumstances, their views and feelings, it is time to examine the role of the 'helping professions' in this aspect of adoption.

Most of the suffering in life is due to events which cannot be changed: the clock cannot be turned back, decisions cannot be unmade. People vary in how they live with painful events. What is gradually becoming more widely understood, however, is that bottling up grief, anger or guilt can be harmful to people's mental – and indeed physical – health, and that it is much better to express and release deep feelings, especially if they can be acknowledged and accepted without accusation and retribution. That is what counselling is all about, and it is significant that it is increasingly being offered in all kinds of contexts and following all kinds of disasters.

However, counselling as it is currently defined is a relatively new concept. As social attitudes became less rigid, particularly in the area of sex, and as the 'stiff-upper-lip' ethos began to be questioned, a recognition began to spread of the common human need to talk about one's distress.

The literature reflects the gradually changing attitudes not only of society but also of professionals towards unmarried pregnancies and single parenthood.

Indeed, in many instances doctors and social workers were ahead of their time in their approach, and what they urged did not always happen. For instance, in 1961 Dr Donald Gough (1971) spoke at a conference on 'Adoption and the Unmarried Mother'. He described his regular visits to a mother-and-baby home, and his observations based on discussions with the young mothers there. He said:

All the girls in the home felt that they had made a 'mess' of things. If such girls are able to understand their own feelings of

107

guilt towards their babies, their parents and society, they will be able to clear up the 'mess', and this is something which is crucial for their future emotional development. I want to consider how adoption, as we practise it, will help or hinder a satisfactory solution of their dilemma. I should like to start with the following propositions:

1. The girls have considerable guilt and depression about the situation they have produced. They would very much prefer to be able to face these feelings and to deal with them, but they are so afraid of doing this that they are tempted to deny both guilt and depression and to blame someone else.
2. Although each girl may have firmly decided in favour of offering her baby for adoption, there is always part of her that wants to keep him.
3. They will have great emotional difficulties about parting from their babies.
4. When they do part from their babies, they need help in mourning their loss.
5. It is quite possible to do the right thing for the wrong reason. We wish to help them to do the right thing for the right reason.

The sentence that stands out in all that is the fourth point, about the help mothers need in mourning their loss. Gough pointed this out in 1961 (Gough, 1971), but throughout the sixties it was common for a mother to receive no further professional help once the baby had been placed for adoption. This was not true of every agency, but offering help in mourning the loss was by no means standard practice.

In 1966, Iris Goodacre published her research study, *Adoption Policy and Practice*. It is significant in itself that this study did not include birth parents, who are really only acknowledged in one paragraph in the concluding chapter. However, this paragraph makes some telling points:

The Hurst Committee recommended that 'children should be protected from unnecessary separation from their parents' and 'natural parents must be protected from hurried or panic decisions to give up their child, and from being persuaded to place them unsuitably'. The law endeavours to protect mothers from hasty action by requiring them to wait until their baby is six weeks old before they can give a valid consent to adoption. But where parents have little opportunity to discuss their plans for the child with a competent person, the value of this safeguard is reduced. Although natural mothers who relinquished their babies were not interviewed, records and other sources suggested that few had been able to explore the alternatives to adoption in this way. In some cases it appeared doubtful whether alternatives existed which could offer a mother sufficient social and financial provision to enable her to keep her child without considerable difficulty. In particular this seemed likely when she could not, or would not, rely upon the assistance of her family. In the eyes of some natural mothers, even the best alternatives available must have seemed unattractive compared with the advantages the child was assumed to gain from adoption. Carefully considered decisions require real alternatives to choose from, as well as competent and timely assistance.

It therefore seems clear that, even at the time, there was evidence that the services birth parents were receiving were less than adequate, whether before or after the birth. Small wonder then if the continuing needs of mothers who parted with their children were not recognized, still less catered for.

THE TIMING OF HELP

However, there is another side to this, which is the difficulty social workers and others have in offering services to mothers who may want only to forget the painful time during which they knew the worker. In her 1971 study of single mothers Raynor wrote:

Only seven mothers had a social worker at the time of the second interview, and these were all girls who kept the baby. Since social workers were identified with this unhappy period in their life, mothers were glad the contact had ended, although a need for further casework and counselling was often apparent to the interviewers ... The problems for the mother in relating to a new agency, or even a new worker, were all too clear, and mothers very often saw the adoption worker as interested only in the baby and not in her. The only adoption agencies which came in for positive comment were those which worked with the mother during pregnancy and continued to give her support and help right through the placement, signing and court hearing.

This ties in with what we have been recognizing as an important factor in the way mothers adjust to the loss of a child. Those who had support and the opportunity to talk about what had happened tended to fare best. Sadly, this seems to have applied to a minority of mothers in any of the known studies, and where it did apply most of the support seems to have come from the informal networks of family and friends. In spite of the quotations above, there is little evidence that professionals, whether in social work or health care, really recognized the deep trauma caused a woman by parting with her child in such circumstances, and because of this lack of understanding no appropriate services were in the past made available.

COUNSELLING AT THE POST-ADOPTION CENTRE

More recently, because of the higher profile gradually being accorded to this side of the adoption triangle, some recognition of the need for services is developing. One exploratory step towards this was achieved when, in 1986, the Post-Adoption Centre was set up in London to offer counselling and family work to any of the participants in an adoption. Birth parents were included in this, although the team of workers had little idea at the beginning about what services would be required or the likely extent of the demand. Publicity about the centre soon brought inquiries from all three sides of the triangle and a clear pattern began to emerge of the feelings and needs of birth mothers.

'I have never talked to anyone about this before,' says a choking voice on the telephone. 'If I ring off suddenly, it's because my son has come in and he doesn't know anything about it.' 'Do other women feel like this – so guilty – even twenty years later?' asks another woman. This sense of great isolation with their feelings was the first thing that struck the centre's counsellors.

Over and over again a woman will say: 'I told my husband before we got married, but we've never discussed it since, and nobody else knows, except of course my parents, and they've never wanted to talk about it.' Or women say, 'I never married, and people think that of course I must be childless, and I never feel able to tell them.' Almost all mothers talk about the effort to cover up the bouts of sadness, depression, anger and, above all, guilt they have experienced. The very fact of seeing a notice offering counselling or groups to women in their position was for some an unbelievable relief – that someone, somewhere, is acknowledging that they have feelings and needs, and indeed that they even exist.

At the time when adoption figures reached their peak in Britain in the 1950s and 1960s, not only was the traditional 'stiff-upper-lip' ethos still very prevalent, but the stigma of bearing a child out of wedlock was very great. 'It has always been the object of the English to be respectable,' wrote Swinnerton (quoted in Bridges, 1956). 'The loss of respectability was an insupportable punishment, amounting almost to physical torture.' If counselling was considered, the emphasis was felt to be on admonitions to repentance and to better behaviour, rather than as an opportunity for the woman to unload the burden of her feelings and to share her pain and grief. Adoption agencies would have tried to help the mother plan her 'return to normal life' but few women report having been given any outlet for their feelings, and few felt they deserved it. Most agencies told mothers they could come back if they needed help, but few ever did. Shocked, bruised, guilt-ridden, most did as their parents and society expected of them, and tried to 'put it all behind them' and carry on with their lives as though nothing had happened. As far as is known, most succeeded, but the cost has never been fully measured. Only now that women are coming forward in sizeable numbers is it possible to begin to learn something of the strain of keeping this burden-some secret.

Counsellors offering a service to birth mothers have to realize that the secrecy in itself has been part of the burden. Losing the child caused most women a lifelong hurt, but added to that has been the shame and guilt which meant it could not be talked about, nobody must know. For this reason, many people are extremely tentative in approaching the Post-Adoption Centre, or seeking counselling elsewhere, and it must be supposed that many never do. Some will telephone with an insignificant, factual question, testing out the reaction and attitudes of the counsellor, before daring to reveal some of the deeper feelings which are really the issue.

Once having taken the first step, however, a woman may find immeasurable relief in telling her story. Whether she tells it in a group of other mothers or to a counsellor on her own, it may be the very first time she has described the whole series of events as she sees it. This in itself can be therapeutic. Putting an order, a logic into what happened, expressing it her way, from her own point of view, reviewing it many years later and above all being listened to and accepted, can be a very reassuring, even healing process. More often than not women cry when telling their story, and are able to release feelings, knowing that others who share them are there and understand, or that the counsellor acknowledges the pain and is not passing judgement or telling her to 'pull herself together'. As one mother said: 'It's good to talk to someone who doesn't say it will all be all right.'

People know the facts cannot be changed, or the child brought back, but they can at least shed the pain and stress of pretending it never happened, of having an important part of themselves and their experience denied. They can be helped to realize that they are by no means alone in what they suffer. Jane said in a group, 'I can at last acknowledge I was a mother – I am a mother – and no one can take that away from me, even if they took away my child.'

One of the difficulties for the mothers, and also for counsellors, is the complexity and the range of emotions that are involved. Sadness, anger, grief, resentment, shame, regret, love and hatred may all have a place, and overriding all is usually guilt. Some of the feelings in themselves give rise to guilt – a woman may feel bitter and angry towards parents who did not support her in keeping her child, but she may not feel comfortable acknowledging that in some way she hates something about her parents, and may guiltily repress those feelings. Learning to live with guilt is not easy. If one can be forgiven, the feelings may gradually ease, but women who have parted with a child can sometimes not forgive themselves, and that leaves the wound open. Many say they hope their daughter or son will trace them when grown-up, so that they can explain everything 'and be forgiven'. The fear that their child will grow up condemning them is very real for many women, and very hard to bear over the years. Others cannot forgive themselves for having meekly accepted parental pressure and parted with their child. Viewed from the greater maturity and security of the present, their submission to such pressure seems incomprehensible, even despicable, and a woman will often castigate herself for not having stood up to her parents, or society, however unrealistic that would probably have been at the time.

With all these feelings, the best help that can be given is to invite their expression and to acknowledge their validity. As with all counselling, reassurance has little place. 'Feeling better' does not happen because people are told to cheer up, or because their actions are said to be justified. People feel better when they feel understood, and cared for, and accepted, and when the pain they feel is acknowledged rather than denied or dismissed. Once they have verbalized it, made some sense of it, most people can gradually start to live slightly more comfortably with whatever their hurt may be. It will not go away all at once, and indeed it may never go away completely. People do not get over the loss of a child, any more than they get over the loss of a limb, but they find better or worse ways of living with the absence.

ROSEMARY'S STORY

Rosemary is an example of a mother who had suppressed all her feelings over the years, and who made a very tentative inquiry before feeling able to risk exposing her suffering. She rang the Post-Adoption Centre in response to publicity about a group for birth mothers, although she knew she did not want to join a group. She asked questions about the sort of people it was aimed at, and what the counsellors planned to do in the groups, and only gradually edged towards saying that she had parted with a child seventeen years previously, and that this was the very first time she had made that statement. The counsellor asked her a few questions about her circumstances, keeping it all fairly factual but trying to convey a sympathetic understanding of how Rosemary must be feeling. She then suggested that Rosemary might like to follow up on this momentous admission by visiting the centre and talking about what it must have felt like to live with such a secret over the years. The counsellor told her some of the things other mothers had said, and suggested that some of them might also apply to Rosemary, which with considerable relief she agreed they did. The conversation ended with an appointment being fixed for a few days later.

When Rosemary came to the centre, she was nervous and shy. She sat on the edge of her chair, sipped anxiously at her coffee and agreed that it was an unfamiliar and uncomfortable experience for her. The last time she had been in a social worker's office was when she parted with her baby. The counsellor guessed how she must be feeling, based on what other mothers had said, and encouraged her to start with a factual account of what had happened to her all those years ago. As Rosemary got into her story, she gradually relaxed and sat back, although her account was punctuated by physical indications of how she was feeling. She became tense at the painful parts, she cried as she described the actual parting from her baby. At first she tried to hold back the tears, but when the counsellor told her it was all right, indeed natural, to cry, she let herself go, and sobbed for several minutes. She then began to apologize, and only half accepted the counsellor's assurance that she had a right to these sad feelings. Rosemary, like so many other birth mothers, had been left with the feeling that she was of little worth as a person, that her feelings were irrelevant and that, if she suffered, it was no more than she deserved.

The story was a sad but very common one: Rosemary had been seventeen when she got pregnant by a boy she had known at school, and had been going out with for about a year. Both sets of parents had been horrified when they heard of the pregnancy, and had forbidden the young people to meet again. Rosemary had been sent away to a mother-and-baby home, where her boyfriend had written to her a few times. She had hoped he would stand by her, and that in the end they might be able to marry and keep the child, but parental pressure was strong, and while Rosemary was away, the boy started seeing another girl. By the time she got home, several months later, he had moved to a job in another town. She never saw him again. Her parents refused to talk about the baby, and made it very clear to her that 'what the neighbours might think' was much more important to them than her need to acknowledge and come to terms with what had happened.

Rosemary did a secretarial training, and worked in an office for five years. She could remember little about those years. They had merged in her mind into a grey, indistinct succession of days through which she had drifted with no sense of purpose and very little enjoyment. She felt as though a vital part of her had died, as though she had had a walk-on part in a play whose plot she never fully understood. After five years, she met a somewhat older man who soon asked her to marry him. She told him about the baby, and he said, 'Well, that's all behind you now', and they never mentioned it again. She had two children of the marriage, and had been tolerably happy, but the births had brought back disturbingly violent feelings of grief, and she found they did not compensate at all for the lost child. She had suffered severe post-puerperal depression, and her life had been punctuated by bouts of unexplained ill health and days of overwhelming sadness. Her husband had been very patient, but she never knew if he realized how much she thought about her first child, and how guilty and bad she felt.

It was clear from Rosemary's account that she had got stuck at the point of mourning the loss of her child. She had had to stifle her feelings. There was nothing that had happened since which had given her the opportunity to re-evaluate the picture she had of herself as a 'bad' person. The counsellor decided to offer her a series of sessions in which they could go back over the whole story, exploring in more detail her feelings at each stage, her relationships and the pressures and influences on her. She could be helped to move forward to the present, where she could see her life as it really was, in the round, rather than dominated by the shadow of the adopted child. The aim was to help her feel and acknowledge the emotions attached to each stage, to see that they were accepted and validated by the counsellor, and then to move on to acknowledge and recognize the other feelings which belonged to the present, putting the past ones in their place, in the past, without in any way denying them.

Rosemary accepted this offer, saying she already felt quite different for having shared her story with someone else. Over the following three months, in fortnightly sessions, she worked hard at the task. She responded well to the opportunity in which she allowed herself to concentrate on her own feelings and need, and to let someone else see them too. By the end, she had resolved to talk to her husband for the first time about the adopted child, and to discuss with him whether and when they should tell their two children, given that once the adopted daughter was eighteen she might choose to trace her mother. Rosemary showed signs of much greater self-confidence and said that the expression of her anger towards her parents which she had allowed herself in the sessions had removed 'a hard, tight little ball' from her middle. She still found it difficult to forgive their attitude, but she felt rather better able to put it behind her and let go of the rage which had consumed her. It was clear that this was only the beginning of a process which Rosemary would need to continue for some time, but it was equally clear that she had been able to free herself from the point where she had become caught, and was well on the way to moving forward into her present world. This did not mean that she was any less sad about her loss, or that the anger and guilt she felt had magically disappeared, but she was able to get them more in proportion, and to acknowledge all sorts of other feelings she had, related to her present life, which also needed to be valued and which were not all negative.

'ADOPTION IS FOR LIFE – BUT IT'S NOT'

As we have heard, one of the things which makes it harder to deal with the grief of a mother who lost a child by adoption is that, unlike death, it is not final. As one mother said: 'There's no body, no burial, no ritual. I walked into an office with my baby, and walked out without her, and that was that.' Women have been expected to go back to work, or to studying, as though they had had chickenpox. There was no public sympathy because usually nobody knew, and any mourning had to be done in secret. Yet the mother felt as though she had been bereaved, believing there was no hope of ever seeing her child again.

When the law was changed by the Children Act 1975, adopted adults gained the right to obtain their original birth certificate. The possibility of tracing their birth mother then became much greater. For many mothers this was a source of joyous hope. For some it brought fear and horror, especially to older women, who had been made to feel such shame and whose secret was probably totally unshared, even by a husband. What the change did do, however, was make the parting less final. How can a mother resolve her grief if she knows that eighteen, twenty or even thirty years later her child may come back into her life? For some it feels better, for others worse. Some say it means they need never really say a final goodbye, hoping that, in spite of the years, it will only be '*au revoir*'. Others say it leaves them in a state of anxiety.

In trying to help women in this position, the main task is to focus on their present reality. This may only be possible after the welter of feelings has been acknowledged, as in the case of Rosemary. It may be necessary to go back over the past, to put some order and sense into it. All that happened cannot be denied or its importance minimized, but the pain is attached to the past, and the person needs somehow to become more grounded in the present. There may be a husband and other children, there may be a job, there may be ageing parents. Whatever the setting, the person concerned may have felt she was not functioning well in it, or was denying part of herself, or going round and round in her guilt and sense of loss. She can be helped to bring out these disruptive feelings, to recognize where they originate and what they are doing to her, and to look at how she could function differently. It will be important to identify what can and cannot be changed, and to look at ways of achieving such changes as can be hoped for. Confiding in someone, confronting someone, simply telling someone how she feels, may seem a big step, but it may bring about change. Distancing herself from the loss, putting it into better perspective, to some extent letting go of the past and concentrating on the present may also be important. Rosemary was helped to do this by seeing the schoolgirl she had been as though on a television screen, 'watching' her go through the parting with her child, and realizing that the adult she now was had come a long way from the frightened, lonely and guilt-ridden young girl she had been. Seeing it all as though at one remove, and describing what was happening in the third person, helped Rosemary to put some of the necessary distance between herself now and the past, and to realize how little choice she really had

had in the final decision. She said she felt better able to leave the feelings of that time around the birth behind her, and to look more honestly at how she now felt.

Another strand of the work consists of helping a birth mother reappraise her own strengths, and look at what has in fact enabled her to carry on with her life. This is not the same as 'looking on the bright side' or counting her blessings, although many do do that. It is an attempt to recognize, and to help the mother recognize, what it is in herself which she has drawn on to combat the pain. Some people respond by saying they have totally failed to do this, and that is why their lives are in such a mess, but it would be rare indeed to meet someone whose strengths had not carried her forward, even if only by virtue of going on living, which some women have gone through phases of wishing not to do. Most can see that in fact they have many qualities which have enabled them to make something of their lives – to give to others, to raise other children – only their own sense of self-esteem has been so low that they have been unable to recognize this. The counsellor's own belief in the ability of human beings to go on growing, emotionally, spiritually or intellectually, is an important prerequisite, along with a belief that people can take charge of their own lives, however hurt they have been. Nobody can cure someone else's emotional pain if that person chooses to hang on to it, but a good counsellor or therapist can offer the tools and the insights to enable the person to reshape their own life and to walk away and take control.

A NEW LOOK AT THE NEEDS OF BIRTH MOTHERS

What seems to be needed, therefore, is a completely new look at the needs of women who part with children for adoption. It must be recognized that such an act has lifelong implications, just as it does for the adopted person and the adoptive parents. Not only must the choices and outcomes be thoroughly explored with a mother, both before the birth and again following it, but she must be prepared for the long-term effects of her decision. She must be offered help to live with it. Much is of course already known about working with bereaved people. What has been highlighted in seeing birth mothers a number of years later is that the only help they may have been offered came at the wrong time. Agencies which tried to give support often did so just when the mother was in the initial stages of shock and often she could not respond. Later, when the numbness wore off and she began to experience the pain of the loss, the grief, the guilt and the need for support in rebuilding her life, it was too late. Contact with the agency had ceased. It would have required too great an effort to remake it herself. Often she felt ambivalent anyway, and believed she was unimportant to the workers whose main interest she saw as securing the baby's future and securing a child for the adoptive parents.

It is noticeable that women frequently cannot remember the name of the adoption agency, or where it was, and many have completely blocked off any memory of the details of that painful time. Words like 'zombie' and 'in a dream' are often used to describe that period, and it is not surprising that any help that was given may have been forgotten, or could not be fully used while the mother was still so shocked.

Agencies will need to recognize all this in their work with birth mothers. They will need to find ways of maintaining contact through and after the period of shock. Agencies will also have to recognize the needs of the thousands of women in the community who gave up children in the past and who did not get the help they needed to cope with their loss. Birth mothers need to know that their existence and their needs have finally been acknowledged, and that they do not need to screw up their courage to ask for something to which they feel they have no real right. This may be particularly true for the black women whose children have been placed for adoption in white families since the late 1960s. Adoption by strangers being an unfamiliar concept in many cultures, black women who had no choice may suffer a double sense of guilt and concern. After years of silence and neglect, these mothers have a right to be heard. The chance to talk, meet other mothers and sit down with a counsellor is an important first step in healing the pain.

8
Not Alone

'There we were – just a roomful of ordinary women. If a stranger had walked in, who would she have thought we were? And yet for us, it was such a momentous occasion.'

'Who we were' was the first group of birth mothers ever to have met in the United Kingdom. Almost all had kept the adoption of their child a complete secret, and had lived with feelings of shame, stigma and guilt. Now for the first time they were sitting round together, talking, telling their stories, laughing and crying, looking just like any other gathering of women with a common interest but feeling they had taken such an enormous step just by being there.

This sense of secrecy and isolation was one of the first things which struck counsellors at the Post-Adoption Centre when they started talking to birth mothers. Although of course each knew she was not the only woman who had ever parted with a child for adoption, she usually felt as though she was, since it was rare to have encountered another woman who acknowledged having done so. It is not something one readily divulges to strangers, or even sometimes to fairly close friends or family. Perhaps this isolation is one of the characteristics of mothers who need the help of somewhere like the centre. People who come to the centre are a self-selected group, and of course little or nothing is known about those who do not seek such services. Some of them may have found an equilibrium simply because they have been able to talk to family or friends or other people.

Recognition of the need to talk, and to realize they were not alone in their experiences and feelings, led to the centre counsellors deciding to offer a series of groups for birth mothers. They did not know what kind of response to expect, nor what the expectations of anyone who came would really be. With some trepidation, but also a great sense of excitement at breaking new ground, they advertised three dates on which any woman who had parted with a child could come along and meet others. These meetings were to be open-ended and exploratory, designed to test out what might be wanted. The impact was in fact overwhelming.

We put out the most comfortable chairs (though we didn't know how many we'd need). We bought flowers, and laid on tea, coffee, fruit juice and biscuits. Then we stood around wondering if anyone would be brave enough to come, and wondering how to put the first one or two at their ease. We had planned how to get the discussion going, using some of the themes which always come up in telephone conversations or interviews with birth mothers. Within five minutes we had abandoned all thought of using these plans. The women who came needed no help to get going. They were just so pleased and relieved to be in a room with other women who knew exactly how they were feeling, without needing to explain or hide anything. Their stories and feelings came pouring out, and we realized that our surmise had been right, and groups were very much what some mothers wanted. We felt a strange mixture of pain at the terrible stories we were hearing and excitement that it was possible for these women to share their pain in this way, and that we had found a way of helping them to help themselves and each other. That first group made a terrific impact on all of us.

Although they had abandoned the original plans for getting the meeting going, the two counsellors involved quickly recognized that it would be necessary to structure the meetings so that there was time in the latter part to move away from the emotional content, and give participants the chance to recover and get back in control before they had to go home. Some found this hard to do, and skipped meetings if they had felt too exposed or vulnerable the time before.

After a false start with the first group, when an unexpectedly large number of people came to the third meeting, the groups tended to be small, ranging from nine or ten people to only three or four. Being small enabled them to become intimate and relaxed, so that participants could get to know each other, and everyone had time to talk. In fact, to ensure that this happened, a pattern developed of operating a 'round', when each member of the group in turn was allotted time to talk about whatever was uppermost in her mind. Some of the topics raised often became the main focus of the subsequent discussion. However, with experience, over four series of groups, the group leaders also realized that there were certain regularly recurring themes, which could be woven into a structure, giving each session, and the overall series, a shape and purpose.

THEMES THROWN UP BY THE GROUPS

The themes fell into four main areas:

1. Grief, loss, anger and guilt, the expression of which usually included a telling of the actual story.
2. The impact of parting with a child on the mother's subsequent life, including her relationships, whether or not she had other children, her sexuality and her health.
3. Concerns about the child while growing up, and the need, indeed often desperate longing, for information.
4. The possibility of being traced by the adult son or daughter – and the desire of some mothers to trace their child.

Obviously it was not always possible to separate out these themes, but each could in turn become the main focus. Depending on the composition of the group, the relative importance of each theme varied. For older women, whose sons and daughters were now grown up, the prospect of being traced, or even of undertaking a search themselves, was often the prime concern. For the younger women this was still a distant prospect, and they were more likely to want to focus on the pain of the separation, their anger and hurt at the way their parents had failed to support them, or had set more importance on 'what the neighbours might think' than on their daughter's or their grandchild's well-being. Many had been left feeling that they themselves were of no importance to anyone, and their sense of self-worth was almost nil. It was painful to admit this but the value of the group was highlighted by the way other women responded. They showed real understanding and they helped boost each other's morale.

This group interaction fully justified the counsellors' original vaguely formulated expectations that many women would benefit from meeting with others. The exchange of stories, the sharing of emotions, the testing-out of reactions and ideas which went on in the groups showed how invaluable the coming together was for the mothers. Leaders and group members were able to reformulate statements so that people saw what they had said in a different light. Things someone had struggled to understand or come to terms with alone suddenly seemed more comprehensible or acceptable when seen through the group's eyes. People began to be able to redefine themselves in the light of this experience.

Sometimes it was not possible for the group leaders to know what was being helpful to someone in the group. It might seem that one member was dwelling rather a lot on some topic, or that the stage another was at was not common to the group, but almost invariably somebody would indicate, either at the time or later, that the contribution concerned had helped her to understand something about herself, or to put something in perspective.

It also often happened that a mother would become very distressed. However, it was clear that from early on most people felt safe to let this happen. They knew that the other women would not only understand but would comfort and often hold them. They would share their pain in a way nobody else ever had. These meetings led to several close friendships being formed, and many mothers continued to meet after the formal groups had ended.

What also happened was that the group gave women who had previously been very isolated a collective voice. For some, this was just a matter of being able to say 'we' rather than 'I' and know that she was speaking for many others who felt the same. For others, it went further, and some collaborated in more educational or political undertakings, beginning to try to make the views and feelings of this side of the adoption triangle heard.

1. Grief, Loss, Anger and Guilt

The first grouping of themes (grief, loss, anger and guilt) were, as might be expected, present as a background to all the discussions, and expressed in a variety of ways. There was always a comparison made with the grief caused by a death, and discussion of how adoption was and yet was not like a bereavement. The lack of public recognition and sympathy was the main feature marking the difference for mothers of adopted children, together with the absence of ritual, and the confusing nature of the 'gone but not dead' situation. One group was particularly conscious of the change in society's attitude to loss, demonstrated by the way widows in the First World War and victims of all kinds of attack and abuse had not been accorded public recognition of their pain, whereas now the victims of disasters such as the Zeebrugge shipwreck or those bereaved in the Falklands war received much public sympathy and support, including counselling.

Anger was felt in varying degrees by the group members, though often its opposite – depression – was very visible. Women were angry with parents, angry with a society which put 'respectability' at the top of its priorities and showed so little forgiveness to those who had behaved in ways which were soon to become the norm, angry with a system which cut them off so completely from their child and treated them so uncaringly. They were particularly angry with the social workers who had been the instruments of society's policies, and although some made exceptions for individuals, most had no good word to say for them. This was, of course, difficult for the social workers running the groups, who did not want to be singled out as exceptions, but who were trying to demonstrate the caring and changing face of social work.

What seemed to give relief to the participants was realizing that their anger was shared and normal. Sometimes a woman would express real hatred for the adopters who had been able to offer her child all she had not been able to, or for the worker who had actually taken the child from her arms. Others would join in, and then they would all laugh, and agree that it was not a personal hatred of these people, but an expression of their overall anger about what had happened.

What was perhaps surprising was the wide variation in degrees of anger felt towards the father of the child who had been adopted. Some women were bitter about the man, and resentful that he had 'got off scot-free' while the mother had had to carry the burden both literally and metaphorically. Often, however, the women were protective of the men, and had been so at the time, refusing to disclose his identity if he had been married, or showing remarkable understanding of his inability to be more involved.

Some were still in touch with the father, or at least knew how to contact him if the adopted young person should come searching and want to meet him too.

The anger which was probably the most destructive was that which had been turned inwards. Most women felt some anger at themselves for what had happened. Some had never been able to get outside that feeling. The self-reproach had turned to self-denigration and despair. Depression had dogged them and had thrown a real blight over their lives. Some were able to use the groups to start the healing process, and to begin to realize that they could overcome this total despondency. A few realized that they needed individual help, and sought further counselling or therapy. For some women, depression had been sparked off after the birth of a subsequent child but, unlike most post-puerperal depression, had failed to go away.

Mingled with all these feelings was the perpetual guilt which birth mothers invariably emphasize when talking about what they have gone through and what they carry around with them. They tend to feel trapped in a double-sided guilt – first for having got pregnant in circumstances which precluded them caring for the child, and then for having 'given a child away'. These were feelings that might never entirely leave them, but what the groups did was to enable them to express how they felt, realize that others felt the same way and receive the solace of total understanding. The groups also enabled women to see how others had coped with their feelings, and what devices each had found for carrying on their lives in as bearable a way as possible.

2. The Subsequent Effects of Adoption

The second theme running through all the groups was the impact on the mothers' subsequent lives of having had a child adopted. A major theme was whether or not a woman had had further children. Some had been unable to get pregnant again. They had had to live with the bitter pain of having parted with their only child. Some had chosen not to have any more children, even on occasion having a pregnancy terminated rather than risk either being the 'bad parent' they felt doomed to be or losing another child by whatever means. Many had married and had more children, but this had not always been unalloyed joy. The second birth had often been a traumatic time, bringing back the pain of the first one. It often required the mother to add yet more pretence to that which she was already living, because this was the first child of the marriage and everyone else was delighted about it. Sometimes there was embarrassment, as when a doctor or nurse openly revealed that it was a second pregnancy, or when there were assumptions made that the mother was inexperienced in childbirth.

There was clear relief in the groups when the members could share such stories, and they suddenly realized that they were not alone in their experiences. Often they could see the funny side of the things which had happened, and in spite of the anguish of most of the participants, there was in fact a great deal of laughter during the meetings. This was particularly so when they shared tales about their experiences in mother-and-baby homes. There was much banter about how they had been in the 'Home for Naughty Girls' or for 'Fallen Women', and they could laugh at what were nevertheless horrific stories of the way they had been treated with a total lack of respect or consideration of their feelings. For some women, this was probably the first time they had been able to laugh at any aspect of what had happened, and this was very therapeutic.

The lifelong impact of the adoption was highlighted in the discussions about subsequent relationships, marriages and children. Feelings about pregnancy or childbirth had often affected sexual relationships, and the knowledge of this previous child had often shadowed a marriage. Having more children could in no way replace the lost child, but mothers had had to keep up the pretence that all was now over and forgotten, and they were content in their new-found respectability.

A further challenge in having subsequent children was whether and when to tell them about the first child. This was the focus of much debate in the groups, and there were no easy answers. Some mothers had told their children as they reached adolescence. Most had not told their children. They struggled with wondering when the best time would be, what the children would think of them, how they could expect youngsters to keep to the straight and narrow if they knew their mother had strayed. Would they feel they too might be 'given away' as the first one had been? Would they be angry at having a sibling they could not know or see? One mother inadvertently told her five-year-old son, and was dismayed when he innocently went round to all and sundry talking about his older brother and causing her enormous embarrassment.

Many mothers felt it was or would be important that children knew about the adopted brother or sister before he or she came knocking on the door, if that were ever to happen. However, having put off the telling until the children were teenagers made it hard to know how to broach the subject. Often there had been no further discussion of the adoption with the husband either. It meant raising it all with him again too. Those women who had been able to talk to their husbands over the years felt very lucky alongside those who struggled to work out the best way to handle the long-neglected subject. The groups provided a forum where these things could be threshed out, and where members could get advice and support from each other.

A further aspect of the long-term effect of the adoption which was much discussed in the groups was the relationship of the mother with her parents. Most of the group members felt that their parents had been unsupportive, and many had been told they could not return home until they had parted with the baby. Although most had been very young at the time, and had been obliged to return home as they had nowhere else to go, relationships had naturally been strained, and sometimes had never recovered. Because women had been made to live a lie, and act at home as though nothing had happened, their whole relationship with their parents became the acting out of a lie. Some had never forgiven their parents for the stance they had taken. Many said they had only a very superficial relationship with them. There were a few women whose parents had understood, and supported them in making a difficult decision, but perhaps by its very nature the group attracted people who had not had a good experience.

Discussion in some groups touched on the kind of mothers those who had borne other children thought they had become. Some felt they had been more detached than they would have liked, particularly with the first child after the adopted one.

Others felt they had been ultra-protective, dreading the loss of a second child, through illness or accident, or whatever. Many had set themselves impossibly high standards as mothers, in an attempt to eradicate the image of themselves as 'failed parents' and to prove that they could bring up a child. Yet others found they could refuse their children nothing, needing to pour out all the love and giving which they had been prevented from bestowing on the adopted child. Many stories were exchanged in these sessions, and without a doubt the members of the group learned a lot about being parents from each other. This was not always easy for those who had not had more children, but even so they could see that having another child had not been any kind of solution in itself, bringing, as it did, its own challenges and dilemmas.

3. Concerns about the Child

The third group of topics centred much more on the adopted children themselves and on the mothers' concern for them. All the women found it almost unbearable that they had not been able to have any news at all of their child once the adoption had gone through. Even one or two who had been promised subsequent photographs or information had often not received it. The most common refrain was 'We don't even know if s/he is alive or dead', and there was always questioning as to whether they would be informed if their child had died. Sadly, the answer had to be 'No', as it has not been agency practice to do this, and anyway the tracing of mothers who had not been asked to keep in touch for this or any other purpose would pose very great problems.

Realizing this often re-emphasized for mothers the feeling they had of being totally negated as people throughout the adoption process. They recognized that the child's needs came first, and often felt they had made the decision for adoption solely to ensure that these were met. However, the system seemed to them, and indeed to the group leaders now they were forced to re-examine it, totally inhumane.

The help people now get after major disasters had been cited as an example of the improvement in understanding of psychological needs, but disasters loomed large for many of the mothers. There were many occasions on which a woman had suffered agonies wondering whether her son or daughter was one of the victims of some major catastrophe. Mothers of sons now in young adulthood had been tormented by the thought that their son might have been in the stadium at Hillsborough, for example; and notices in newspapers of a child dying in a road accident often led to women trying to work out if the age was exactly the same as their child's. The worst aspect of all this was the not knowing. There was widespread agreement that any dreadful fact could more easily be faced than horrible fantasies.

Those whose children had been of mixed parentage (there were no black women in the groups, but the fathers of some of the children had been black) had yet other concerns about their child. Mostly the children had been adopted by white parents, and the mothers wondered if they suffered from racism as they were growing up, or whether their black heritage was being acknowledged or valued, or just denied. Sometimes the child's colour had been the reason the mother's parents had been unable to accept the child, and this was a source of additional anger, pain and guilt for the mother, who also wondered whether the adoptive parents would really be free of such prejudice.

Concerns about these unknown people who were bringing up their children were voiced a lot by some groups. The women knew that adopters usually had to prove they were infertile before being accepted, and there was speculation about how this might affect their parenting or their relationship as a couple. The knowledge that they themselves had at least been able to bear a child was for some women a wry kind of comfort when they thought about the paragons of virtue to whom their child had been entrusted, who had passed every test as prospective parents and been given the gold seal of approval. All had been made to feel that, whereas they had earned society's opprobrium by their conduct, adoptive parents represented all that was desirable and good. In fact, it was quite hard for some women to realize that, in spite of all the procedures, adoptive parents were just people like anyone else, and that their child might not have had the idyllic childhood they had comforted themselves they had made the sacrifice for. In one group there was clearly considerable discomfort when this idea began to be formulated. People did not much want to dwell on it. The parting had only been bearable because the mother thought her child would not only have two caring parents, but security and happiness almost of a fairy-tale kind. The thought that the adopters might have divorced, died, been poor parents or in some other way have let their child down was almost unbearable to some.

4. Tracing

The importance of being realistic about the kind of lives their children might have had became particularly apparent when the discussion turned to the topic of being traced by the adult son or daughter. For the older members of the groups, this was not only a realistic possibility, but in some cases it had already happened. In the smaller groups, where perhaps only one woman had had this experience, she found it hard to keep a balance between meeting her own need to work out what the experience meant to her and not rousing too much envy from those not yet at the stage where this could be hoped for or, indeed, putting people off by highlighting some of the potential difficulties.

A few women had themselves found ways of undertaking a search for their now adult son or daughter. This was the source of enormous interest in the groups. Some women were envious, some thought they would be too scared of disturbing the adoptive family's life, some were worried about what they might find. Others felt that, as the adopted person had the right to search, the choice should be his or hers, and they would wait to be found. Many had no idea that they could lodge information with the General Register Officer, the adoption agency and NORCAP (National Organization for the Counselling of Adoptees and Parents) to make their child's search easier.

There was considerable debate about the legal and moral 'right' to trace adopted children. Almost all agreed that it was best to wait until the child was an adult, and accepted that the age of eighteen, when adopted people gain the right to their original birth certificate, seemed appropriate. To many, however, the fact that this right was one-sided, and birth parents had no access to information about the identity of the adoptive family, seemed very unfair. They were indignant at the assumption that they would rush in and upset everybody, or try to take back their child. Some expressed the view that the law seemed to assume that birth mothers remained for ever the immature, irresponsible young girls they were thought to have been at the time of the birth, while adopted people and presumably also adoptive parents matured and reached a point when they could handle the facts about the original identity of the child.

This assumption also coloured relationships with authority generally. Some had approached the original adoption agency, or the social services department, for more background information than they had been given at the time about the family which adopted their child. Sometimes they also wanted to know if there had been any more recent information about their child. Often they felt the reception they got was suspicious or even hostile, and that they were not being credited with any kind of sensitivity or maturity. There were, however, exceptions to this. One woman had a thoroughly positive experience which affected all her group. Her son had been adopted some eight years previously, and she had mourned his loss ever since. She felt she had never been able to make anything of her life, although she was a very able person. Coming to the group gave her the confidence to write to the adoption agency and ask if there was any more information she could be given, to put her mind at rest. She came to the following meeting looking euphoric, with a letter which gave her a lot of non-identifying information about her child and his family which was totally reassuring. The social worker had included details which meant a lot to the mother, such as the things the boy was good at at school, activities he had recently mastered and traits which his mother could see might be inherited. What the letter also achieved, however, was the final realization on the part of the mother that this was in fact no longer her child, but was a little boy who was well integrated and happily settled in his adoptive family, and in whose present life she could play no part, nor he in hers. Far from adding to her despair, this knowledge and understanding freed this woman to begin looking at her own needs and her own life, and in fact she finally found the energy and impetus to fulfil a lifelong ambition to go and work abroad. Her friends in the group all felt this was a wonderfully positive outcome.

What this also highlighted for the group leaders was the value of information at a later stage. Without this letter, that particular woman might never have been able to reconcile herself to what had happened. There must be many others who would be both comforted and helped in the detachment process by being able to know how their child is faring. The desperate need for a mother to try to trace her son or daughter might also be allayed if information were available about him or her.

Mothers who had been traced had experienced a wide range of reactions and events. One or two were still in the early stages of euphoria. For some, there is the danger that the intensity of the relationship can lead to sexual expression. For others, the contact with their son or daughter had settled down and become more relaxed. And there were a few who had really got into the doldrums. It seemed in some cases that the searching son or daughter had been little more than curious, and had not followed up the contact with any real effort at forming a relationship. This had been extremely hurtful to the mother, who had herself tried to keep the contact going, and felt very discouraged if there was no initiative taken by the daughter or son. Discussing some of these complications in the group certainly alerted other members to the possible difficulties if their own child ever sought them out.

A common fear of group members in talking about being traced was that they might find they had little in common with their child. Differences of class, of attitude and expectations were all possibilities, and one of the biggest fears was that the mother might be rejected once found. To her, this would be a second failure to 'measure up' and most women thought it would be devastating. Most of them hoped to have the opportunity to explain what really happened and they also wanted reassurance that they had in fact done the right thing, and that their child's life had been happy. Some wondered about their relationship *vis-à-vis* the adoptive parents and what the role of each would be once the adopted person knew them both.

Another issue was that of the place of the child's father. Mothers assumed that they were likely to be questioned about this, and in most cases they would in fact be the sole source of information about the father. It would be difficult to know how much to tell, and to sort out questions of confidentiality versus the son or daughter's need to know about their origins.

Present partners also came into the discussions. Most knew of the child's existence, but there had often been no subsequent discussion. Would it be better to alert a husband to the fact that the adult child might come searching, or to wait till it happened, if it ever did? Should they be involved in a meeting when it happened? Some were said to be very supportive, to know the mother was coming to these meetings, and to be encouraging of them. Others had more difficulty with the whole topic, and tended to indicate that it was their wife's affair. If the daughter or son did turn up, this could be difficult to handle. At least discussion in the group meant that these particular women would be rather better prepared if a reunion did occur, having had time to think about it and to glean ideas from each other. They also clearly felt that there would be support available if they needed it, either from other group members or from the Centre's counsellors.

OPENING UP ADOPTION

Underlying all these topics of discussion and concern were some general issues of a fundamental nature. What the group members were often really asking in a variety of ways was: 'What *is* our place in the so-called "adoption triangle" and do we really matter to anyone other than as the bearer of a child?' What, they wanted to know, could be done to change public attitudes to mothers who lost their children through adoption? Whether or not it had been forced upon them, most of them felt they had made the greatest sacrifice they could be called on to make, in their child's interests, and they resented bitterly still being made to suffer the censure of a hypocritical society. They also wanted the lifelong implications of the decision they had made to be understood, and for the helping professions to offer them the same support that others who are bereaved or in trouble seem to get.

Looking to the future, group members gave considerable thought to how adoption could be opened up, to get away from the total secrecy which used to surround it and which led to such suffering. They all favoured the possibility of an exchange of information via the adoption agency over the years, so that either party could ask for it if they wanted, but it need be imposed on no one. They especially wanted the agencies to become more aware of the needs of birth mothers over time, and not to see the relinquishment of a child for adoption as something which could be put behind one, and gradually forgotten.

The counsellors running the groups invariably found them intensely moving and indeed draining experiences. Deep emotions were finding expression, often after years of being pent up, and it was important for the workers to remain detached in order to be helpful to the group. There was no doubt of the importance of having uninvolved group leaders, who could hold things together if they really began to get out of hand, and to give a sense of structure and security to the participants.

Attending a group had often been only the start of the search for help, and a number of the members subsequently sought personal counselling at the Centre, or therapy elsewhere. This seemed to the leaders very appropriate, since the groups could often only set in motion a process which might need a lot more private work before it could reach a satisfactory conclusion. There was however no doubt about the enormous value of the groups, and of bringing together women who had such a fundamental experience in common and who could do so much to support and succour each other.

9
Coming Full Circle

CHILDREN SEEKING MOTHERS

'I don't think anyone else in the world could be so happy,' wrote Joan when her son, aged twenty-seven, traced and made contact with her.

'I don't know how you found me, but I don't ever want to hear from you again. I don't know anyone of that name,' said a tense voice on the telephone. A counsellor at the Post-Adoption Centre, acting as an intermediary, had written a disguised request for contact with the birth mother of an adopted young woman, and this was the initial response.

These polar reactions, and all those in between, are now familiar to counsellors and others acting as intermediaries, although the negative responses are considerably less frequent than the positive ones. Even people who have expected or perhaps longed for contact find that, when it happens, it is a shock, and produces a depth of emotion for which they could not prepare. Some say the range of feelings, and their strength, are only equalled by everything they felt at the time they first parted with the child. In some instances, these feelings have had to be smothered on both occasions, because, for example, other family members do not know about the child, and this adds to the strain and the turmoil.

Tracing birth relatives has been a possibility in England and Wales only since 1975, when the Children Act gave adopted people the right to obtain their original birth certificate after reaching the age of eighteen. In Scotland, access to the original birth records had been a possibility right from the first Adoption Act in 1930. Access to the original birth certificate is a prerequisite to a search for most adopted people, since the majority do not know their name at birth, nor that of their mother. Once they know the name, and also the address at the time of their birth, which may or may not prove useful, and also perhaps the name of the adoption agency which arranged their placement, adopted people have a good foundation for starting a search. Some take years to complete it, whether because it proves so difficult or because they choose to leave time between each step and only move gradually towards a conclusion. Others throw themselves into it with tremendous energy, and cannot rest until they have located their mother. How they then choose to make the approach can be crucial to the outcome.

I got a phone call from my mother saying this girl called Tina was looking for me. She said her mother had been at school with me and had asked her to look me up. My mother hadn't given her my address, but took a number where I could ring her if I wanted to. I knew immediately who it was. I don't know if my mother suspected. We've never talked about my daughter since she was adopted. I couldn't stop shaking. I walked around the house in a tizz, couldn't sit down, couldn't think straight. Thank goodness she didn't just arrive on the doorstep. I couldn't have coped at all. As it was it took me three days to get myself in a calm enough state to make that phone call. I had to tell my husband or he would have thought I'd gone mad. We'd never really talked about my daughter, though I'd told him about her before we got married. I hadn't told our children, and we decided it was better to wait until I'd met Catherine (I still think of her as that) before working out what to say.

Very different in approach was Marie, who telephoned her birth mother, established who she was, and said, 'I think you're my mother.' Dorothy was very shaken, but did not deny it, and agreed that Marie could come and see her. She had remained single, so at least did not have the complications caused by the involvement of husband or children. Marie came, told a long story of an unhappy adoption and being misunderstood by her parents, and made Dorothy feel desperately guilty and unhappy. After several meetings Marie indicated that she wanted to move in to live with Dorothy, and Dorothy felt too guilty to resist, although she felt very uncomfortable about it. When she finally got in touch with a counsellor because the arrangement was not working out and she did not know how to handle it, she said that in fact she felt the person who most needed help was Marie. She felt the whole thing might have worked out differently if she had been warned of Marie's wish to see her, known something of the background and been able to prepare herself for the contact.

John's approach was different again. He used an intermediary to make the initial contact with his mother, who was then aged sixty-eight. John had waited a long time to begin searching, and had only done so after the death of his adoptive parents. In response to the first, disguised letter to his mother, the intermediary received a phone call from a friend of the mother saying the latter had been very distressed by the letter she had received, and did not wish to reply. The friend did not seem to know what it was about, so the intermediary had to be very cautious in what she said. She asked the friend to say that a response of any kind, even with news of her health and welfare, would mean a great deal to the originator, and please to get in touch if ever she felt she could. Meanwhile there was no intention to intrude or upset her. Months went by, and then shortly after John's birthday a phone call came from his mother. She told the intermediary that she had known who it was trying to contact her, but had been so devastated that she had been unable to respond. For fifty years she had tried to put her son out of her mind, and the shame and guilt she had been made to feel had never really gone away. The letter had thrown her into a state of total confusion, in which visions of the baby she remembered intermingled with the image of a middle-aged man arriving and calling her 'Mother'. She was a widow, with two married daughters who knew nothing of her son. She had agonized over how to tell them, and how much it would upset everybody to know her long-kept secret. She was not sure any good could come of a meeting, and yet as the weeks passed she realized how deeply she longed to see this son and to explain to him what had really happened. In the end she overcame her qualms, and allowed John to visit her. The 'hour over a cup of tea' lengthened into a four-hour visit, and was followed by many more, as a mutually deeply rewarding relationship developed, and enabled the mother to brave the world and acknowledge this long-lost son.

Other older women do not overcome their fears and worries, and refuse ever to meet their daughter or son. This is much less common in younger women, but after perhaps forty or fifty years of suppressing their feelings, and at an age when it is getting harder to adapt to new things, some cannot bring themselves to turn their worlds upside down. The older the mother, the more likely it is that even her husband may not know about the adopted child, and the idea of his finding out after all these years is unthinkable. What anguish these mothers suffer by being sought we do not know, since they usually make it clear they want no further contact with the intermediary or the person concerned.

Even mothers who are glad to have been traced report how confused they found themselves at first. Most of the emotions they have repressed over the years have been negative: guilt, sadness, anger and grief. Suddenly there comes the relief of at least knowing that their child is alive, and that the possibility exists of actually seeing him or her. Then comes the realization that it is a twenty-, thirty- or forty-year-old person they are talking about, not the infant they remember; a stranger, not really a daughter or a son; someone else's grown-up child. How will the adoptive parents feel about the contact? There is all the worry about how people in the birth mother's own circle will feel or react: parents who probably knew about the baby at the time, and may have insisted on the adoption; husbands or partners; subsequent children; friends and neighbours – the supposed opinion of the latter so powerful in the pressure for adoption in the first place. The surge of joy alternates with fears of all kinds. 'Is he angry with me for giving him away?' 'Will she understand the pressure I was under?' 'What if he hasn't been happy?' Sometimes there is a strand of resentment: 'I have finally got my life together, and put that behind me, and now here it is, bang slap in the middle of my life again, churning everything up, forcing me to face the world with my life an open book.'

Many mothers talk of living suspended between two worlds, desperately trying to reconcile the revived emotions of the pregnancy, birth and separation with those of the present, the sorrow of the missing years with the joy of a prospective reunion. 'I couldn't sleep,' wrote Miranda. 'I had to get up and walk around the house. I would sit over a cup of tea, do the ironing, my mind in a whirl. But somehow it was easier to begin to sort it all out at night, when there was no one else about. I needed time. I am so glad Mark could be patient, and didn't push me to meet instantly.'

Miranda and Mark exchanged letters, then photographs, then more letters, for more than two months, until Miranda felt ready to meet. She felt a neutral place was important, and chose somewhere totally secluded, where they talked non-stop for five hours. She was overcome by Mark's likeness to his father, and this threw her into even more of a state of confusion, as she see-sawed back and forth between her own young self and the maturity of her actual age. The dominant emotion was joy, but she said the 'shock and muddle' in her mind took a long time to settle down.

PLAYING FOR TIME

Needing time to adjust, to think, to sort out one's feelings is a very common phenomenon in the course of a reunion. Perhaps because, however much it may have been longed for or even half-expected, the contact when it does come is a shock, people often seem to need a breathing space before responding or being able to decide what to do. Barbara was located by her daughter after a very brief search, and was sent a letter through an intermediary. When this brought no response, a second letter was sent, suggesting that the first one might have gone astray and sending a copy. Barbara was also assured that if the contact was seen as intrusion, it would not be pursued, but the writer needed to know. This letter brought a warm response, saying that it was not unwillingness but a need for time which had delayed the reply. Jill, the daughter, then wrote directly, and was disappointed when again it took several months for a reply to come. This was the pattern throughout all the early contact, and it took a year to reach the point of an actual meeting. Barbara was affectionate and concerned when they did meet, and a good relationship was subsequently established, but she said she could not have rushed into it. Jill found the delays frustrating and puzzling and wished she could at least have had some explanation as time passed.

Veronica, on the other hand, caused her birth mother equal heartache by her slowness to follow through on her first contact. Having met her mother, she was taken aback by her lifestyle and the many differences between them. She did not regret having found her, but needed time to absorb what she had found, and there were long gaps between their meetings. Her mother found this very frustrating, and kept ringing Veronica or writing her letters, begging to meet. Veronica enjoyed the meetings when they did take place, but said that one lasted her a long time, and she always wanted space to think about it afterwards.

DIFFERING EXPECTATIONS

One of the greatest risks in reunions between adopted people and their birth relatives is that the expectations of the parties involved may not coincide. This can cause untold distress for either or both, and is again something for which it is very hard for people truly to prepare themselves.

Betty was traced by her twenty-five-year-old son without much difficulty. He had married two years previously and had a baby daughter. His wife had pressed him from the start to find out more about his background, and had taken a lot of the initiative in the searching process. Betty, who had remained single, was overjoyed to be found, and to discover that she was a grandmother. She loved visiting the little family, knitted clothes for the baby and very much envisaged becoming a regular part of their lives. Only gradually did it dawn on her that she was making all the running; rarely did they actually invite her to visit, or telephone her. They were polite and welcoming when she rang or visited, but it became clear that both the other sets of grandparents were actively involved, and that it was becoming quite difficult to find a place for her. She realized that her son had been mildly curious about her and his background, his wife perhaps more so, but now that their curiosity was satisfied, they were not particularly interested in more than a very tenuous relationship with her. This realization was a bitter blow to Betty, whose new-found sense of self-worth and satisfaction in life evaporated completely. She felt deeply hurt that the past had been raked up again only to present her with yet more pain. She thought perhaps she was being punished for rejecting her son by now experiencing this rejection herself.

Janet, on the other hand, came to feel suffocated by the demands and attention of her daughter Tessa, who was twenty when she found Janet. Tessa had had a stormy relationship with her adoptive mother, and although the last two years had been calmer, she found it very pleasurable to have a daughterly relationship with someone who had not been involved in the past history. She would telephone Janet at all hours, or arrive unannounced, and pour out long tales about her latest boyfriend, her job, her shopping expeditions, the films she had seen. Janet, who at first had been delighted by the contact and to know that Tessa was alive and well, began to find the intensity of Tessa's attachment very difficult to handle. She did not want to make her feel rejected, but she felt that her life had been invaded and taken over, and moreover by a young woman she increasingly came to see as extremely self-centred and not particularly likeable. Janet was hard put to it to find ways of gently creating more distance between them, and she was also very saddened to realize that the daughter she had dreamed about so often over the years was not at all like her dream in reality.

This kind of difference of expectation – of the kind of person the other may turn out to be – is not uncommon. However hard they may try, it is impossible for adopted people not to have certain expectations about what their birth parents will be like, just as it is for the birth parents. Having met each other, they may find that, whatever they knew intellectually before, they are still surprised, pleased or disappointed by what they find. Even after the exchange of photographs, the height of someone may be surprising, or a young person may be taken aback at the signs of ageing in someone whose age they actually knew. More important, there may be differences of class, education or interests which make it hard to establish a real rapport, once the first euphoria of meeting is over.

DEVELOPING A RELATIONSHIP

Difference of lifestyle or background need not always make for a distant or difficult relationship. Godfrey had been adopted by an upper-middle-class family who had sent him to public school and university, and he was well settled in a respected profession. When he found his mother she was working as a school cleaner, and had never had much education. For them, this was not what mattered. They warmed to each other immediately, became exceedingly proud of each other, and found a sense of humour in common which led to hilarious meetings. They were soon able to establish a pattern of regular visits which both enjoyed and which appeared remarkably uncomplicated.

Not all relationships develop so easily, however satisfying they may turn out to be in the long run, and it is clear that the more preparation both sides can have for the meeting, the more likelihood of success there is. This is another argument in favour of using an intermediary in making contact. The intermediary can help each party prepare for what to expect and if it is someone who regularly acts in this capacity he or she can draw on previous experience to help both people really think through the issues. Minimizing the initial shock and reducing the chance of a door being slammed in someone's face is only part of the story. Working out the subsequent relationship is a much longer-term exercise and there are sure to be many ups and downs along the way.

There appears to be a certain pattern to what happens in the early stages of developing this new relationship, although each one will be unique and there will be many variations. It seems, however, that the early days are usually characterized by a mixture of shock and euphoria on the part of the birth mother. Many speak of being on a 'high', on cloud nine, over the moon. Excitement, relief, joy, are overriding emotions. In time, however, a more mundane sense of reality begins to take over, and the need to integrate this new relationship (if there is to be one) into the person's everyday life becomes apparent. This is when the temperature may drop, and reactions set in. The mother even feels quite depressed for a while. It may also be a time when a little of the edge is taken off the happiness of knowing that the daughter or son is alive and well. They may recognize that their child has faults and shortcomings. Established relationships may come under pressure. Expectations, each of the other, differ. This is when the hard work of sorting out what kind of relationship is possible and desirable must begin.

Perhaps the greatest difficulty is that there is no blueprint for such relationships – no socially accepted definition of role or outline of how to behave and where the birth mother fits in. The adopted person may feel a conflict of loyalties. The birth mother may not want a mother's role but yet want recognition and a place in her daughter or son's life – but what place? Some bend over backwards not to appear a rival to the adoptive mother. Others feel the adoptive mother has had twenty or thirty years of the 'child' and now it is their turn. Adopted people may find it difficult simply allocating enough time to everyone who wants it. One young man, whose adoptive parents had divorced and each remarried, and who had traced his birth parents who were each married to someone else, found his time cut out trying to spend Sundays or weekends with 'each of my four mothers'!

The reactions of family members on both sides may exert a strong influence on the new relationship and how it develops. For instance, birth mothers who married after the adoption, and maybe had other children, often find handling the knowledge of their adopted child with their family difficult. Most will probably have told their husbands but often there will have been no subsequent discussion. Many will not have told their other children. So when an adopted son or daughter enters the scene, there will inevitably be a number of hurdles to jump in deciding who to tell, when to do it and how.

Marjorie had told her husband about her son, and on rare occasions he had been mentioned, but the three children of the marriage knew nothing. When Ben made contact, Marjorie immediately told her husband, and was relieved that he was so understanding and supportive. They agreed to tell the children, now all teenagers. Marjorie found this an agonizing prospect, fearing what they would think of her and dreading their censure, both for having had an illegitimate child and then for parting with him. She also thought it made all her attempts to encourage them to behave responsibly look very hypocritical. However, she steeled herself and cried with pleasurable surprise when all three showed nothing but sympathy and understanding. They were then quite cross with her for having expected anything else. They were excited and curious to meet their unknown elder brother, and urged their mother to move quickly to a meeting so that they too could be involved.

Once the meeting had taken place, Ben was soon welcomed into the family, where his uncanny likeness to the middle son could not go unnoticed. The early meetings were exciting for everybody, but then Marjorie began to realize that the eldest of the three, a girl called Emma, was jealous and unhappy. She finally confessed that she minded no longer being the eldest, she minded her mother having had such a major secret she had not shared and she minded all the fuss and attention Ben was getting when there were concerns of her own which she wanted her mother to notice. Marjorie felt very guilty, realizing that in her own joy she had not paid sufficient attention to how the advent of ᵗhis son might affect all the other members of her family. It took time, a lot of talking, some spacing out of Ben's visits and a conscious effort on everyone's part to restore a balance of relationships. It helped Emma when she realized that Ben himself had brothers and sisters in his adoptive family, and was not really looking for a whole new family for himself – a close friendship would suffice. He also had a good relationship with his adoptive parents, and although knowing Marjorie was immensely important to him, he was not expecting her to become his mother in the sense in which she was Emma's.

Unfortunately, not everyone is as balanced or mature as Ben, and sometimes the relationship with a new-found family can be much more difficult. Karen bounded into her birth mother's family with enormous enthusiasm, welcomed by a euphoric mother and an enchanted husband, who went to all lengths to make her feel one of the family. Karen did not have a very close relationship with her adoptive parents, and as an only child had always longed for brothers and sisters. Finding several of these was a delight to her, and she showed little sensitivity to the feelings of these other young people. Margaret, her birth mother, was blind for a long time to what was happening, so thrilled was she to have found her daughter and so guilty did she feel to learn that the adoption had been less than happy. Gradually, however, it dawned on her that her other children not only resented this newcomer but did not even like her. They resented the time, energy, devotion and money being lavished on her by Margaret and their father. It took a long time for all this to be sorted out, and the eldest child left home well before she might otherwise have done, to Margaret's great sorrow.

It is often very hard for mothers who have lived with the guilt of having parted with a child to refuse them anything when they first reappear. Usually the mothers are in far better circumstances than at the time of the birth, and they are able to provide in a way which was impossible when they were much younger. Their guilt makes them feel unable to do anything which might be felt as rejection. A number of mothers have sought advice from the Post-Adoption Centre when the going gets difficult, knowing what it is they ought to do, yet feeling the need of outside approval and even 'permission' to free them to do it.

SEXUAL ATTRACTION

Probably the last thing in a birth mother's mind when she is facing a reunion with a son or daughter is any thought of sexual attraction, but there is increasing evidence that it can play a part, and that people need to be warned about it. Perhaps because the emotions on finding each other are so powerful and perhaps because the adopted person or the mother wishes, however unconsciously to recapture the physical contact between mother and baby, a birth mother can find herself drawn into a sexual relationship with her adopted child. She may become swamped by the explosive mixture of love, desire, guilt and confusion.

Deborah was seventeen when she gave birth to Andrew, and thirty-six when he traced her. She was petite and pretty, and he was a tall, well-built nineteen-year-old. When they met, Deborah said the shock nearly caused her to faint – here was Andrew's father reincarnated, just as she remembered him at the time of Andrew's birth. Even his voice was the same. Andrew was someone who liked to touch and to hug people, and in no time at all the intensity of their emotions had led them into each other's arms and then into bed. Deborah felt it must be wrong, but everything in her drew her to Andrew and she felt quite unable to stop herself. While she agonized Andrew seemed cheerfully unconcerned, and took every opportunity to be with her. A break only came when Andrew's work took him too far away to be able to see much of her, and Deborah sought help to break out of what she saw to be an impossible situation.

In some instances the powerful sexual attraction, combined with a lack of emotional control, has led to violence. More than one young man has become so obsessed by his feelings for his birth mother, and so devoured by the need to make up for the missing years, that he has terrorized her with his possessiveness and jealousy, and brought havoc into her life. Guilt again had a large part to play in these circumstances, because the mother felt unable to stand up to her son in the obvious way. She was unwilling to reject him again. One mother was so bothered by the guilt she felt when she became sexually involved with her son, seeing no way out of it, that she committed suicide.

These are extreme cases. The vast majority of adopted people who develop a relationship with a birth relative do not become sexually involved. However, it illustrates the strength of feeling that can be aroused when mothers meet sons or daughters that were last seen as babies.

THE DEATH OF A BIRTH MOTHER

It is not known how many mothers have died, taking their secret to the grave, and never experiencing the joy (or the trauma) of a meeting with their child. Certainly, for the searching adult to reach the end of their quest only to discover that the parent has died can be a bitter disappointment. It brings a twofold sadness – for the death itself and for the loss of an opportunity to meet the parent. Some people are angry with themselves for not starting the search sooner; some feel betrayed by the parent, as people often do at a death. Sometimes there is the added hurt that other people do not seem to understand the sense of loss. Ursula reported that her friend said, 'Well, it's lucky you didn't know her – you can't really mourn for someone you don't know.' For Ursula, that was the ultimate incomprehension. She had longed all her life to know the woman who gave birth to her, had searched for her for years and had felt devastated when she finally learned that her mother had died a good many years previously. She said she felt more bereaved, not less, for not having had the opportunity of knowing this parent.

Sometimes people are able to meet and get to know other relatives – children or a spouse of the dead parent, brothers or sisters, uncles or aunts. On occasion this has been a helpful experience in coming to terms with the loss. Martin found that his mother had died of cancer two years before he traced her. His mother's husband seemed to understand very well his frustration and sense of loss, and spent a long time digging out photographs for him, and talking to him about his mother. This was a far cry from Jennifer's experience. She approached her aunt, the sister of her birth mother, to ask if she could have a photograph, and was treated as a liar and an impostor, and forbidden to contact the family ever again. Jennifer was so upset and demoralized by this that she gave up the attempt to go further, even though other relatives might well not have treated her in the same way.

MOTHERS SEEKING CHILDREN

Many people feel that the Children Act 1975 did not go nearly far enough in its provisions for access to information for people involved in an adoption. Many birth mothers feel it is unfair that adopted adults should be able to know their identity and trace them, but that there is no reciprocal right. They feel they were not consulted about the change in the law, and there were those among them who did not welcome it. If there are adopted people or adoptive parents who would not welcome birth parents having equal rights, should their view carry more weight?

Some women have felt freed by the change in the law from their commitment to lifelong ignorance of the fate of their child. Very few indeed want to intrude on their child or the adoptive family's life, but many desperately want to know what happened to their son or daughter, and some have taken steps to find out. In some cases, adoption agencies are understanding and helpful, and have agreed to approach the adoptive family for news of the child concerned. This at least protects the family's anonymity, and provides an intermediary in the transaction. Other agencies tell the mother that the door must remain closed, and that they can neither provide nor obtain more information. In some cases, this has been conveyed in such a way as to harden the determination of the mother to take matters into her own hands. Alison said that if the agency worker had even seemed to see her as a person, and recognize her long-standing anguish and her need to know, instead of treating her much as she had been treated when an errant schoolgirl mother, she might not have felt driven to undertake an actual search. However, she did, and ended up by finding out where her daughter lived and worked, with the accompanying joyful relief of knowing she was alive and doing well. She decided not to make contact at that point, but to give her daughter more time to reach the point of wanting to make a search herself. Alison had made it easy for her by notifying her address to the General Register Office, the adoption agency and NORCAP, which runs a contact register through which not a few reunions have been brought about.

Comparatively little is known about the outcome of reunions which have been achieved by a birth parent taking the initiative. The numbers are not very large. In the absence of the adoptive name it is extremely hard for a mother to trace her child. Those who have enough information to get started may have felt guilty about taking an action to which they have not specifically been given the right. However, a number of such reunions are known, and predictably they cover a wide range of outcomes similar to those in which the adopted person has sought the reunion.

Jennifer was devastated by her daughter's furious refusal to meet her. Margaret was so thrilled by the warm response she received from her daughter that she wanted to find a way to help all birth mothers to trace their children. Anne suffered agonies because she did not really know where she stood. Her daughter seemed pleased to have met her, responded whenever Anne suggested a meeting or wrote to her, but she never initiated any contact. Anne never felt sure how welcome she really was. Her long-standing guilt over relinquishing her daughter was now converted into doubts about whether she had done the right thing in tracing her.

The 1989 Children Act made provision for an official contact register to be set up by the General Register Office; this register enables both relatives and adopted adults to notify their interest in contact with the other party. When there is a 'match' the General Register Office notifies the adopted person. The provision came into force on 1 May 1991. However, many people feel it does not go far enough and that equality requires the giving of permission to birth parents to trace their daughters or sons as adults, and therefore to have access to their adoptive identity once they are eighteen.

CONCLUSION

Whatever the legal developments, there is no doubt there has been a fundamental change in the way many birth mothers view adoption. Whereas probably every mother in the past really did think she had seen the last of her child, many now know or believe that they will meet again in adulthood. The range of responses to this possibility is wide. There are some mothers who part with their child because it is the only thing to do as far as they can see, and who feel able to live with their decision. There are those who will suffer as much as the older women have. They will wait with impatience until the passage of time permits the possibility of a reunion. At least, since the change in the law, mothers enter marriages or relationships aware that their child may trace them later. Social attitudes have changed enough for there to be less stigma attached to both illegitimacy and parting with a child for adoption. Greater openness and possibly better facilities for exchanging and updating information between adoptive and birth families may mean a greatly reduced need for the kind of anguish described in these pages.

10
Reshaping the Past, Reforming the Future

We have seen that women who become pregnant find that their experiences of childbirth and motherhood are as much a product of the way people around them react as they are of the biological event itself. The pregnant fifteen-year-old is regarded very differently from the married woman in her mid-twenties about to have her first child. What for the one is a time of upheaval, worry and guilt is for the other a period of satisfaction, pleasure and achievement.

The physical accomplishment is the same for both women. However, the social circumstances under which it takes place are entirely different. It is socially expected that a young married woman should have children. When she is pregnant, everyone is pleased. In contrast, the young unmarried woman is not expected to have children. If she does have a baby, few people, if any, will congratulate her or celebrate the child's arrival. She is not thought fit either to have children or to rear them. She has done wrong and will continue to do wrong by keeping the child. It seems that the only way for her to right the wrong is to give up the child and return to being a single, childless woman. Although she will suffer the pain of losing her baby, she will enjoy a return to social acceptability. However, other people may not be so forgiving. Having given up her baby, she is liable to be condemned both as a mother who failed her child and as a woman who gave away her baby. When prevailing attitudes are hostile and condemnatory, the mother will feel shame and guilt. Her self-esteem will plummet. She will see herself as a social failure. And on top of all this, she will have lost her baby. The devastating psychological impact of such a damning social reaction to an inherently natural and worthy achievement is not something from which most women easily recover.

It is hard to step outside the way things are. We take our world for granted and rarely question the fairness of it all or wonder who has decreed that things should be this way rather than that.

If you are seventeen, at school, pregnant, and the year is 1968, then it seems that there is no way out of the situation except to have the baby adopted. However, we have to keep reminding ourselves that the way these matters are managed and the way people react are not social inevitabilities. At every turn in the story, things could be different. Unmarried and unpartnered women who have babies could pass without social comment; their births could be occasions for joy like any other. Money and a house, community support and friendly help could be given as a matter of course, forestalling the need for the mother even to contemplate giving up her baby. If the mother cannot look after the child herself – she is too young or unwell – then the baby could be looked after or adopted by other parents, but not exclusively and not anonymously. This is an argument for adoptions which are 'open'. The birth mother does not lose all contact with or knowledge about her child. This reflects changes in what people now think is best for the psychological development of the adopted child. Many believe it is emotionally easier and healthier for the child to have an open, clear and above all real picture of his or her birth mother rather than have her remain a mysterious or forbidden figure. The mother's sense of loss is diminished; the feelings of guilt are assuaged. Her experiences of motherhood and adoption are less traumatic and altogether more comfortable.

Our argument has been that the personal experiences of the mother who places her child with other parents is in large measure socially constructed. Different people at different times in different places have held particular views about the unmarried mother and her child. The mother understands what she has done and what she must do in terms of the ideas of her time. For some, to be unmarried and pregnant is a straightforward and happy experience. Mother and baby may stay together or they may live separately but remain in regular and relaxed contact. For others, to be unmarried and pregnant is a major problem. The mother has fallen short of what the community expects of a young woman. Her behaviour may need explanation. Experts of the time may say that she is bad or immoral, mentally dull or psychologically disturbed. Not only would such a mother be unfit to look after a baby, for the sake of the child she must surrender all her maternal rights. She therefore experiences herself as a morally or psychologically flawed person.

Socially, things can always be arranged differently and this leads to different personal experiences. None of these changes is much use, however, to the mother who gave up her child in days when moral codes were strict and social standards unbending. For hundreds of thousands of women, the clock cannot be turned back. Their feelings of loss and guilt, anger and despair were shaped by a climate of censure and punishment. The only way that these mothers can move forward is to re-examine their experiences, both past and present. By describing what happened at the time, by recognizing how her thoughts and feelings, judgements and decisions were shaped by those around her, she can begin to unravel the various threads that constituted her identity and emotional state as an unmarried mother. By understanding more fully who she was and what had happened, the mother can change the meaning which she gives to her experience. The sequence of examination follows an increasingly clear path. First, the mother remembers and recognizes what she thought and felt at the time. She reawakens old memories; she revives long-buried feelings. Second, the mother reflects on and understands why things happened in the way that they did. She ponders the role of parents, friends and professionals. In such ways, she gives voice to her unspoken feelings, she can allow herself to be angry as well as tearful. She can compare herself with others, for now she knows she is not alone.

In short, the birth mother can examine her life, take it apart, see what it is made of, and begin to put it together again as *she* would like it to be. Having had a large part of her life defined for her by other people, she now needs to build a life of her own. Experiences that were socially constructed are first deconstructed and then finally reconstructed in the light of the mother's examination of herself and the people around her. At a critical time in her life, other people seemed to be in control. By their reactions, through their advice and using their power, they seemed to propel her into a nightmare. The mother seeks to regain control over her own life and resume responsibility for the meaning she gives to her own experience. She needs to work out who she was and what she did before she can decide who she is and where she must go. Such reconstructions take place when birth mothers talk to counsellors. They occur when women meet other women who have lost a child to adoption.

FROM SOCIAL PRESSURES
TO LEGAL JUDGEMENTS

Although there are still young women who give up their babies for adoption, their numbers are now relatively few. It is much less likely that a woman in her teens will find herself pregnant. The average age at which a woman has her first child has risen steadily year by year and typically the first-time mother will now be in her mid-twenties. If she is single, there is less pressure, social or economic, to give up her baby.

The birth mothers described in these pages, though still a sizeable proportion of the female population, are unlikely to reappear in such large numbers again. But they do have their successors. In many ways, these new childless mothers are different. The life of the new birth mother is likely to have been harder and more mean. There are two main groups. There are mothers in Bolivia and Brazil, India and the Philippines whose children have been adopted by parents in the West. We know next to nothing about their lives either before or after the loss of their child.

In the countries of the West, there are an increasing number of women who lose their children through the lawcourts. Experts and welfare officials judge that some children are suffering emotional or physical harm in the care of their parents. These children are removed compulsorily and 'freed' for adoption. The children tend to be older. In professional circles such children have been described as 'hard to place', but with the fall in number of babies available for adoption and through the determined efforts of social workers, more and more of these older children are finding new homes. Over the last ten years many studies have been completed to determine how successful is the adoption of the older child. A good deal is known about these children and their new families, but we know very little about the birth mother the child left behind. It is the child's future welfare that is of interest and not the mother's. The story, of course, is familiar. It mimics the history of baby adoptions in which we learned a lot about the fate of the growing adopted child but knew next to nothing about the birth mother, who simply faded from view. The suspicion is that the traumas and stresses suffered by this new birth mother are very similar. But there are differences.

In the case of the older child, there is a long-standing relationship with the mother. Parent and child have a history, no matter how disturbed or deprived or sad, which cannot be denied. It will certainly not be forgotten. The birth mother's loss is enforced. The relationship between mother and child is ended because other people have decreed it. This increases feelings of anger and helplessness. It is harder to resign yourself to a decision that was not of your own choosing. The traditional birth mother was a product of a particular social and moral climate. Parental and professional opinion about what was best for the baby may have brought pressure to bear on the young mother, but the decision to relinquish the child remained hers, even though many felt that in reality they had little choice. The modern-day birth mother and her experiences are more likely to be the product of a legal judgement. She is officially assessed as unfit to be a parent. Whereas the traditional birth mother had failed as a parent by giving her baby away, the new birth mother has her child taken away because she has failed as a parent. Socially and psychologically, her life is very different from that of the woman who felt that she had no choice but to surrender her baby for adoption.

The typical mother described in this book was still living at home in not unpleasant surroundings with the prospect of education and/or a career ahead of her. The woman who loses her child now does not live with her parents. She is often struggling in an unsettled or even violent relationship with a man who may or may not be the father of her children. Very often it is her choice of partner (an aggressive man) and his behaviour rather than her own suspect parenting that is the cause of the child's removal. After a history of disturbance and deprivation, the final blow for the mother is to lose one or more of her children. It may be that the child is safer and developmentally better off living with other parents, but the question remains whether or not the mother should lose all contact with her child. The loss, for both parent and child, may be more traumatic if it is thought to be final and absolute. Put like this, the new birth mother may earn less sympathy than her traditional sister, but her experiences deserve similar understanding. To lose a baby by death is hard, to give up a baby for adoption is difficult, but to have a child with whom you have lived for several years removed against your will is peculiarly painful.

RESHAPING THE PAST
AND REFORMING THE FUTURE

We have recognized two ways in which the meaning a mother gives to her experience can change: the political and the personal. Changes in adoption policy and practice can create a more open, less punitive relationship between mother, child and adopters. Meeting other birth mothers and talking to specialist counsellors helps those who have already lost a child by adoption to develop a better understanding of what has happened to them and their lives. Rather than see their individual probems as personal failures, they recognize their troubled lives as a reasonable response to a very difficult situation and an extremely painful experience. Their private troubles arose out of social practices. They can begin to learn that their personal hurt and shame and guilt was not a result of their own deficiencies but a product of other people asserting their moral code. The sexuality and reproductivity of women have always been of major concern to men. When women behave 'incompetently' or 'unacceptably' in these matters, they are judged either to be a problem or to have a problem or both. It is by these same social measures that women learn to judge themselves. They understand their own behaviour in terms which are not of their own making. Their experiences are formed by the attitudes and social arrangements of others. In recognizing how others have shaped the way they have defined themselves, women may begin to recover some control over the meaning which they give to their own lives.

Changing adoption policy and practice looks to the future. It aims to prevent women suffering to the extent they have in the past. By listening to the stories told by mothers who have lost their children we may offer the women of the future who cannot care for their children a kinder and more humane treatment. The feminist method gleans 'political insights from an analysis of personal experience' (Collins, 1986, p.215). And by listening to the stories told by mothers who have lost their children, we also help them make sense of their painful past. 'For the first time in twenty years,' said Iris, 'I talked freely. It was a great relief. I remembered things that I had not thought about for a long time. I think I had pushed them to the back of my mind. It was upsetting at the time, but I felt as though a great weight was lifted from me, and the guilt I had suffered for years did not seem so bad.'

REGIONAL POST-ADOPTION SERVICES

ENGLAND

After Adoption Manchester
12 - 14 Chapel Street
Salford, Manchester M3 7NN
0161 - 839 - 4930

After Adoption Yorkshire & Humberside
80-82 Grove Villas, Cardigan Road
Leeds LS6 3BJ
0113 - 230-2100

Durham Diocesan Family Welfare Council
Agriculture House, Stonebridge
Durham DH1 3RY
0191 - 386 - 3719

Merseyside Adoption Centre
316 - 317 Coopers Building
Church Street, Liverpool LI 3AA
0151 - 709 - 9122

Nottingham After Adoption Support
517 Aspley Lane
Nottingham NG8 5RP
0115 - 980 - 4819/4820

Post-Adoption Centre
5 Torriano Mews, Torriano Avenue
London NW5 2RZ
0171 - 284 - 0555

West Midlands Post Adoption Service
92 Newcombe Road, Hansworth
Birmingham B21 8DD
0121 - 523 - 3343

WALES

After Adoption Wales
Unit 1 Cowbridge Court
58 - 62 Cowbridge Road West
Cardiff CF5 5BS
01222 575711

NORTHERN IRELAND

S.& E.Belfast Health & Social Services Trust
1 Wellington Park, Belfast BT9 6DT
01232 381 - 505

SCOTLAND

Family Care
21 Castle Street Edinburgh EH2 3DN
0131 - 225 - 6441

Scottish Adoption Advice Service
16 Sandyford Place, Glasgow G2 2NB
0141 - 339 - 0772

A stamped addressed envelope is appreciated by all these organizations if you write with an inquiry.

Adoption counselling is now required to be provided by local-authority social services departments. You can find the address under the name of your county or borough council in the telephone directory.

OTHER USEFUL NAMES AND ADDRESSES

BAAF (British Agencies for Adoption and Fostering)
Skyline House, 200 Union Street
London SE1 OLY
Tel: 0171-593-2000

Birth-link (Scotland)
Family Care
21 Castle Street
Edinburgh EH2 3DN
0131 - 225 - 6441

Contact Register
General Register Office (Adoption Section)
Smedley Hydro
Trafalgar Road
Southport, Merseyside PR8 2HH

Natural Parents' Network
10 Alandale Crescent
Garforth, Leeds LS25 1DH
Tel: 0113-286-8489

NORCAP
112 Church Road
Wheatley, Oxford OX33 1LU
Tel: 01865-875000

Bibliography

ARMS, SUZANNE (1975) *Immaculate Deception: A New Look at Women and Childbirth*. Boston: Houghton Mifflin.

ARMS, SUZANNE (1983) *To Love and Let Go*. New York: Knopf.

ARMS, SUZANNE (1990) *Adoption: A Handful of Hope*. Berkeley, California: Celestial Arts.

BENET, MARY KATHLEEN (1976) *The Character of Adoption*. London: Jonathan Cape.

BRIDGES, YSEULT (1956) *How Charles Bravo Died*. London: Jarrolds.

BURNELL, G., and NORFLEET, M. (1979) 'Women who place their infant for adoption: a pilot study', *Patient Counselling Health Education* 1, pp.169–72.

CARTER, APRIL (1988) *The Politics of Women's Rights*. London and New York: Longman.

CHEETHAM, JULIET (1977) *Unwanted Pregnancy and Counselling*. London: Routledge & Kegan Paul.

COLLINS, B.G. (1986) 'Defining feminist social work', *Social Work*, May–June.

DEYKIN, EVA Y., CAMPBELL, LEE, and PATTI, PATRICIA (1984) 'The postadoption experience of surrendering parents', *American Journal of Orthopsychiatry* 54 (2) April.

EHRLICH, HENRY (1977) *A Time to Search*. New York and London: Paddington Press Limited.

FISHER, FLORENCE (1973) *The Search for Anna Fisher*. New York: Arthur Fields Books.

GILL, DEREK (1977) *Illegitimacy, Sexuality and the Status of Women*. Oxford: Blackwell.

GILLIGAN, C. (1982) *In a Different Voice: Psychological Theory and Women's Development*. Cambridge, Mass: Harvard University Press.

GOFFMAN, ERVING (1963) *Stigma: Notes on the Management of a Spoiled Identity*. Englewood Cliffs: Prentice Hall (Harmondsworth: Penguin Books, 1968).

GOODACRE, IRIS (1966) *Adoption Policy and Practice*. London: Allen & Unwin.

GORDON, TUULA (1990) *Feminist Mothers*. London: Macmillan.

GOUGH, DONALD (1971) 'Adoption and the unmarried mother' (originally written in 1961) in Tod, Robert, ed., *Social Work and Adoption*. London: Longman.

HELMRATH, THOMAS A., and STEINITZ, ELAINE M. (1978) 'Death of an infant: parental grieving and the failure of support', *The Journal of Family Practice*, 6, 4.

HOUGHTON REPORT (1972) *Report of the Departmental Committee on the Adoption of Children*. London: HMSO.

INGLIS, KATE (1984) *Living Mistakes: Mothers Who Consented to Adoption*. Sydney: George Allen & Unwin.

ITV (1990) *Somebody's Children: Losing*, 26 April (television programme).

JONES, W.C., MEYER, H.J., and BORGATTA, E.F. (1966) 'Social and psychological factors in status decisions of unmarried mothers' in Roberts, Robert W., ed. (1966).

KELLMER-PRINGLE, MIA (1972) 'Making adoption better', *New Society*, 29 June, vol.20, no.509.

KIRK, DAVID, and McDANIEL, SUSAN A. (1984) 'Adoption policy in Great Britain and North America', *Journal of Social Policy*, vol.13, no.1, pp.75–84.

KRONICK, JANE COLLIER (1966) 'An assessment of research concerning the unmarried mother' in Roberts, Robert W., ed. (1966).

LASLETT, PETER (1980) 'Introduction: comparing illegitimacy over time and between cultures' in Laslett, Peter, *et al.*, eds. (1980).

LASLETT, PETER, OOSTERVEEN, KARLA, and SMITH, RICHARD M., eds. (1980) *Bastardy and its Comparative History*. London: Edward Arnold.

LIFTON, BETTY JEAN (1979) *Lost and Found: The Adoption Experience*. New York: Dial.

LIGHTMAN, E., and SCHLESINGER, B. (1982) 'Pregnant adolescents in maternity homes' in Stuart, Irving R., and Wells, Carl F., eds. (1982).

MACFARLANE, ALAN (1980) 'Illegitimacy and illegitimates in English history' in Laslett, Peter, *et al.*, eds. (1980).

MACINTYRE, SALLY (1977) *Single and Pregnant*. London: Croom Helm/Routledge.

NAGEL, T. (1979) 'Moral Luck' in Nagel, T., *Mortal Questions*. London: Cambridge University Press.

PAUKER, J.D. (1969) 'Girls pregnant out of wedlock' in *Double Jeopardy, The Triple Crisis, Illegitimacy Today*. New York: National Council on Illegitimacy.

PINCHBECK, I. (1954) 'Sexual attitudes to problems of illegitimacy', *British Journal of Sociology*, no.5, p.309.

RALL, MARY E. (1961) *Casework with Parents of Adolescent Unmarried Mothers and Potential Unmarried Mothers*. New York: Child Welfare League of America.

RAYNOR, LOIS (1971) *Giving up a Baby for Adoption*. London: Association of British Adoption Agencies, November.

REICH, DIANA (1988) *Working with Mothers who Lost a Child through Adoption*. London: Post-Adoption Centre, Discussion Paper.

ROBERTS, ROBERT W. (1966) 'A theoretical overview of the unwed mother' in Roberts, Robert W., ed. (1966).

ROBERTS, ROBERT W., ed. (1966) *The Unwed Mother*. New York: Harper & Row.

ROCKEL, JENNY, and RYBURN, MURRAY (1988) *Adoption Today: Change and Choice in New Zealand*. Auckland, New Zealand: Heinemann Reed.

ROLL, SAMUEL, MILLEN, LEVERETT, and BACKLAND, BARBARA (1986) 'Solomon's mothers: mourning mothers who relinquish their children for adoption' in Rando, Therese A., ed., *Parental Loss of a Child*. Illinois: Research Press Co.

RYNEARSON, EDWARD K. (1982) 'Relinquishment and its maternal complications: a preliminary study', *American Journal of Psychiatry*, March.

SACHDEV, PAUL (1989) 'The triangle of fears, fallacies and facts', *Child Welfare*, vol. LXVIII, no.5.

SEGLOW, J., PRINGLE, M., and WEDGE, P. (1972) *Growing Up Adopted: A Long-term National Study of Adopted Children and Their Families*. Windsor: NFER.

SHAWYER, JOSS (1979) *Death by Adoption*. Auckland, New Zealand: Cicada Press.

SOROSKY, ARTHUR D., BARAN, ANNETTE, and PANNOR, REUBEN (1978) *The Adoption Triangle*. New York: Anchor Press/Doubleday.

STEARNS, ANN KAISER (1989) *Coming Back*. London: Methuen.

STUART, IRVING R., and WELLS, CARL F., eds. (1982) *Pregnancy in Adolescence: Needs, Problems and Management*. New York: Van Nostrand Reinhold.

TIZARD, BARBARA (1977) *Adoption: A Second Chance*. London: Open Books.

TRISELIOTIS, JOHN (1973) *In Search of Origins*. London: Routledge & Kegan Paul.

TRISELIOTIS, JOHN (1989) 'Some moral and practical issues in adoption work', *Adoption and Fostering*, vol.13, no.2, pp.21–7.

VAN KEPPEL, MARGARET (1986) 'How dare they? The experiences of women who have relinquished children for adoption and the tasks of intervention' (paper presented at the 4th National Women and Therapy Conference, Perth, Australia, 11 and 12 August).

VINCENT, CLARK E. (1966) 'The unwed mother and sampling bias' in Roberts, Robert W., ed. (1966).

WALBY, CHRISTINE, and SYMONS, BARBARA (1990) *Who am I?* London: BAAF.

WEIR, S. (1968) *A Study of Unmarried Mothers and their Children in Scotland*. Edinburgh: Scottish Home and Health Department.

WELLS, CARL F. (1982) 'Introduction' in Stuart, Irving R., and Wells, Carl F., eds. (1982).

WINKLER, ROBIN, and VAN KEPPEL, MARGARET (1984) *Relinquishing Mothers in Adoption: Their Long-term Adjustment*. Melbourne, Australia: Institute of Family Studies.

YELLOLY, MARGARET (1965) 'Factors relating to an adoption decision by the mothers of illegitimate infants', *Sociological Review*, vol.13.

YOUNG, LEONTINE (1945) 'Personality patterns in unmarried mothers' in Roberts, Robert W., ed. (1966).

YOUNG, LEONTINE (1954) *Out of Wedlock*. New York: McGraw Hill.

FOR THE BEST IN PAPERBACKS, LOOK FOR THE 🐧

In every corner of the world, on every subject under the sun, Penguin represents quality and variety – the very best in publishing today.

For complete information about books available from Penguin – including Puffins, Penguin Classics and Arkana – and how to order them, write to us at the appropriate address below. Please note that for copyright reasons the selection of books varies from country to country.

In the United Kingdom: Please write to *Dept E.P., Penguin Books Ltd, Harmondsworth, Middlesex, UB7 0DA.*

If you have any difficulty in obtaining a title, please send your order with the correct money, plus ten per cent for postage and packaging, to *PO Box No 11, West Drayton, Middlesex*

In the United States: Please write to *Dept BA, Penguin, 299 Murray Hill Parkway, East Rutherford, New Jersey 07073*

In Canada: Please write to *Penguin Books Canada Ltd, 2801 John Street, Markham, Ontario L3R 1B4*

In Australia: Please write to the *Marketing Department, Penguin Books Australia Ltd, P.O. Box 257, Ringwood, Victoria 3134*

In New Zealand: Please write to the *Marketing Department, Penguin Books (NZ) Ltd, Private Bag, Takapuna, Auckland 9*

In India: Please write to *Penguin Overseas Ltd, 706 Eros Apartments, 56 Nehru Place, New Delhi, 110019*

In the Netherlands: Please write to *Penguin Books Netherlands B.V., Postbus 195, NL-1380AD Weesp*

In West Germany: Please write to *Penguin Books Ltd, Friedrichstrasse 10–12, D–6000 Frankfurt/Main 1*

In Spain: Please write to *Alhambra Longman S.A., Fernandez de la Hoz 9, E–28010 Madrid*

In Italy: Please write to *Penguin Italia s.r.l., Via Como 4, I-20096 Pioltello (Milano)*

In France: Please write to *Penguin Books Ltd, 39 Rue de Montmorency, F-75003 Paris*

In Japan: Please write to *Longman Penguin Japan Co Ltd, Yamaguchi Building, 2–12–9 Kanda Jimbocho, Chiyoda-Ku, Tokyo 101*